DARK PSYCHOLOGY

MASTERY

2 BOOKS IN 1

Dark Psychology

And

Mind Control.

FRIEDRICH LLOYD

DARK PSYCHOLOGY

Secret Persuasion Techniques to Influence People: Mind Control, Manipulation, Hypnosis, Deception, Brainwashing, Dark Seduction, Dark Triad

FRIEDRICH LLOYD

Table of Contents

INTRODUCTION

Dark psychology is the demonic attribute through which persons manipulate and marginalize other person's identity and cultural values. The arts and tactics through which the person is manipulated contain the use of obscene language, pre-planned unethical gestures, evil diplomatic maneuvers, malicious propaganda and many more. These tactics work on contrary basis to creativity. According to Cropanzano (1999), dark psychology is a mode of applying worst creative means in order to enslave the conscience of a normal personality. This means that if the person is under a trap of dark minds and negative people, then the bad people will use bad omens and gestures in order to embed the mind of the pure person in treachery and theft. This can be done through false propagation of information and other information outlets.

For instance, the person has not committed murder and his nemesis plot something vindictive for him through propaganda and he falls in it then this gesture will be considered a dark psychological motive for the person, who is in shambles now. There are many personalities or entities that fall into the definition of dark psychologists and there are enlisted as follows:

Definitions

The definitions can be enumerated as follows:

It is the study of human nature, in which the predatory aspects of human nature are properly studied. The humans that tend to do sophisticated gestures in order to attain are salvation are defined as dark people. It is the potential of a human race to carefully exterminate the sources of all humans in the world and with the passage of time, it gives the human the value and credit that it wants. Therefore, the demonic nature of human is comprehensively examined in the aspects of dark psychology and all those frontiers of human genome that create a militaristic, antagonistic and harmful nature of the human beings are thoroughly processed in this endeavor.

According to Michelle Rec (2009), dark psychology is the study of all those evil thoughts and norms that cater to the upbringing of negativity in a person's mind and soul. All those perceptions and visual imaginations that compel the human to be treacherous in their time are considered as dark perceptions and their study is dark psychology. The contours of dark psychology believe that the evil mindsets, prevalent in dark minds, have a motivational goal and aim in their minds. Due to which the dark people are considered heroic and nice in their pursuit of things. In order words, dark psychology is a religious zeal given to a human due to which he is able to do bad things in the world.

Furthermore, dark psychology carefully constructs this notion that the dark people also have a vision in this world. It believes that the thought process of individuals compels them to think bad about the omens of society and with the passage of time, they become very malignant towards their goals. They think of negativity as a positive gesture and this style is depicted as malicious and malignant in its way. There is precipitation of thoughts that create deviance in the individuals and he is able to nurture obsessive remarks about everything in the society. This process is called dark continuum, which is the perpetual harboring darkness in a person's mind. There is also a dark factor, embedded in the conscience of humans, which compels them to think and do dark in the coming time.

The concept of dark psychology is easily found in every region of the world. From cultures to religions, from valleys to continents, every person is prone to do something dark in his life. There is a side, which forces and lurks to darkness in the individual, and the individual is prone to do bad things. This is the dark syndrome, which again solidifies the concept of evilness and evil in a person.

Dark psychology further omits this assertion that they are people that want to do such things for the sake of their own interests. They do not want to do it for sex, retribution, murder, revenge and anything evil rather they only want to imbue havoc in the region. This concept is illustrated as dark proceeding, in which the person is able to do dark things on the cost of self-interest and self-salvation. This is the potential to defame and harm others without the explanation of other things to the individuals. The psychology is the emphasis to this credit that the person is able to do harm things just for the sake of fun and amusement.

Also, there is an unnecessary culture of repulsion or impulsion on humans due to which he is not able to share the actual reasons of his frustration and agony but he is repulsive enough to conduct the dark actions with full zeal. Such a culture or attitude is named as Dark mobility in which the person acquires mobile action in order to attain better and productive means of darkness in him. This culture creates a source of repressiveness in the individual and he ultimately creates an aim and a goal, in which he has to do dark things in order to secure and successful.

Humans tend to evolve with time but under the constructs of dark psychology, humans' beings have to be in a zone of antagonism and frustration due to the emblem of dark psychology. The dark psychologists decipher the definition of human beings in a pertinent manner and they are constructing the true nature of human beings that beings are the mythical survivors of the past and they have to do something devastating, in order to survive the horizons of the present. There is a continual set of predatory impel behavior that focuses on the advent of mischief and darkness in a person's mind. This mindset is carefully deciphered in the context of Dark psychology and the person, who is inflicted by it is bound to suffer from the paths of chaos and destruction. All this is implemented due to the edifice of dark psychology.

Many psychologists believe that man is an apex predator. The human being is rational enough to confess the harms of brutality in himself and he is able to practice it, once he is on a spree of dark psychology. The context of dark psychology easily personifies the mode of brutality for the individuals. As he is revolved by the idea of evil and mischief, he has no one to justify or advocate the love of purity. He deems all such rationales to be the utterly disgusting and with the passage of time, he is able to be in cognizant of all the harms of brutality and darkness in the society. Thus, the psychology behind dark psychology is the ability to do bad things in its constructs of positive manner.

Darwin always believed that evolution is the process that makes the better of all individuals. However, in the context of dark psychology, the person is able to manifest the contours of dark psychology in the evolving phase of human beings. The people are not able to pursue the harms and whims of positivity and they all are bound to fail in the contemporary. Therefore, the evolving mechanisms of the people are not able to create good tendencies of affiliation in them.

In the emblem of dark psychology, the person wants to imbue harm in the humans without any positive rationale. This means that the person, who is being dark has no proper justification to induce harm and horror in the society. The person feels very melodramatic while he is under a dark spree and has no sense of affiliation for the person, who are around for him in the society. This is called a culture of deviance and violence due to which, the person is able harbor darkness for the persons and can be malignant in his cause and constructs. Also, the people, who are embedded and engreatened by a notion of darkness, they are ought to come in the negativity of character. They have no sense of logic and proper conviction of doing things that they do and thus, they suffer collaterally in the end.

People, who are clouted by dark psychology are deemed to be unpredictable and unreasoning. The persons, who are dark are bound to suffer from the horizons of devastation and they can come up with malignant intentions and gestures. An analogy can be constructed here in order to understand the meaning of unpredictable darkness. The dark values tend to disgruntle the character of the individual and the individual is not able to go on a rationale of purity and affection. Thus, the culture of unpredictability is harnessed in an individual while he is under the clout of dark psychology.

Dark psychology tends to boost the quality of future exploration in an individual. It is true because while a person is inflicted by the harm of dark psychology, he is not in a personal capacity of engaging in the mind of the public and wants to simply surf on the context of realism and selfish motives. He is not aware of the happenings in the present and he wants to do things by himself. In doing things, by himself he tends to dislocate his aspiration with the present and focuses more and more of the future. Why he does that? Because he wants the result to appear and he does not care about the processing of the present. Therefore, it is pertinent to understand that how psychology, in terms of dark avenues, is applicable to the living of a frustrated mind and how it processes the tours to think more of a futuristic guy.

Tenets of Dark psychology

Following are the six tenets of dark psychology

1. Dark Psychology is universal in its nature

This claim asserts that dark psychology is universal and needs to be implemented at a bigger level. No human being is immune to the dark conduct of life and he has to inflict pain on others just to exhibit a source of retaliation for the other individuals. Initially, he tends to be vindictive. However, with the process of time, he become more lenient and effective. But one thing cannot be ignored that dark psychology is prevalent in modern and post-modern times and with the evolutionary crux of time, the human tends to be sadistic in its actions and gestures.

2. Dark psychology is the study of human condition

The dark psychology is the study of human condition and the condition does not necessarily have to be normal. The condition can be haunting and can be very managerial in its constructs as well. However, one thing needs to be understood carefully that the human condition has to be averse and adamant to evilness. This means that while studying dark psychology, one has to keep in mind that dark psychology will inculcate a bad and worse human condition in them with the passage of time.

3. Dark Psychology is replete of destructive behaviors

The dark psychology has a concept of destruction that makes the human go beyond the character of positivity and purity. The individual is not able to have a stable concept of calmness and acceptability in it and have to be more lenient in order to understand the edifice of love. The individual faces some deep shrouds of destruction in him and this is the most devastating feature of dark psychology in him. Therefore, this tenet needs to be comprehensively manifested for the proper extermination of bad feelings in an individual.

4. Dark Psychology plants out a range of inhumanity

The dark psychology is manifested in terms of inhumanity. The persons that do inhuman acts are bound to constructed in the name of dark psychology. The dark psychology tells that persons are the apex predators of the human nature and they can only evolve in the making, if they tend to be more delinquent in their constructs. This means that only that person can survive, who has the ability to rise against the odds and wants to be more compelling in its nature. Therefore, the term dark psychology can also be described in the mode of inhumanity.

5. All people can be violent

The other tenet of dark psychology is that every human, who breathes and has a predilection to do anything will tend to be violent. This is the inherent quality of any individual and regardless of his and hers intention, the individual needs to ascribe with the violent tendencies. Therefore, this tenet advocates that all people have to be very mature and strong when it comes to the acceptance of violent tendencies.

6. Dark psychology needs to be properly learned

This tenet of dark psychology advocates that in order to know the harms and ills of dark psychology, one has to be in cognizant of its progression. Dark psychology can start its journey as an effective wave of catastrophe and if not tackled with proper care then it can be very harmful for the people as well. In order to make a staggering impact on the halt of dark psychology, one has to eliminate any such mental or emotional prognosis that can lead to the emanation of darkness in oneself.

Other modes of dark psychology

There are many other modes of dark psychology that need to be described as well in order to get a close look in the dark methods of psychology.

1. Dark Continuum

The dark continuum is a set of imaginary lines and circles through which the public is able to get a dark side of almost everything. These circles are based on thoughts, feelings and perceptions that can lead to the task of sadistic ion by a dark body. Once you are in this circle of violence, you are not able to feel purposeful or have any sort of ambition and aim in you. The psychological maneuvering of dark psychology can lead to mental past of illusion and fragmentation that can be horrendous in their making.

2. Dark factor

The dark factor is an apparent real of possibilities and potentials that are provident in all forms of humans. The dark factor will make you feel terrible at times when you are morally or socially dysfunctional. The dark factor can even welcome a spree of negativity upon you due to which you will feel ashamed and be in shambles. The dark factor can cause a lot of tensions and agitation for you as well. Therefore, the dark factor is a dark emblem, which is stored in us and could lead all of us to horror and terror.

3. Dark singularity

The dark singularity is a concept which will be related and comprehended in terms of Astro-physics and astrology. The singularity is a small and dense particle of the dark hole, which is present in the center of the hole and it has a minimum space of energy in it. The dark singularity believes that persons, who are inflicted by it are bound to suffer from the horrors of isolation and estrangement. There are at par with every condition of life and there is a considerable amount of distance in between them and the space that is coming to them.

The History of Dark Psychology

Science has always been questioned with the justification for peace and ethical standards. In the medieval era, the quacks used to heal others by looking at their concealed body parts and sometimes, even sexually insulting them. The practice was later strengthened in the ecclesial order, where clergies would often breach the privacies of individual by giving justification that they are helping others. With the advent of science and technology, precarious missiles and warfare machineries were brought to amazement, which had a sole intention of killing the people. There were debates advocating their pertinent need but only at the cost of thousand of killing, they were created. Thus, psychology, which is also an offspring of science can be interpreted as cruel outlet of science and there are many historical case studies, which led the prelude of dark psychology. These are as follows:

Freud's interest in Young Woman

This was the experiment that was conducted on the behest of Freud's relations with young women. In his Dark continuum, Freud believed that women, who do excessive masturbation are designed to be bad in nature and this is an ill-coordinated exercise that needs to be stopped. His experiments were many young women and out of them, was a young lady named, Emma. Emma had the problems with anxiety and depression and she used to do a lot of masturbation just to make the pain go away and ace the mental trauma. She decided that she will never ever dare to pursue a relationship and in order to ace herself, she went for a doctor, who happened to be Freud. Freud made her inhale serious nostril drugs, which made her go dizzy and how was she treated, remained a mystery for long. The concept of dark singularity can be seen in these experiments, where Freud is testing the enduring skills of Emma and wants to carry on the experiment at the cost of every result.

Electroshock Therapy on Children

Dr. Lauretta Bender of the Creedmoor Hospital believed that children, who do not have any social order in their characters are prone to be tested under an electroshock machine. She would invite many students to her lab and would not see the problems of the children clearly rather would ask some tough questions that would draw children towards confusion. When the children won't be able to answer it then she would put them under an electroshock computer and with the passage of time, the children would lose their subconsciousness and be paranoid. This aspect, according to Dr. Lauretta was a tool to make the children active and strong but, in its progression, the experiments proved their worth. Instead, piles of bodies of dead children became the terrible outcome of such results.

Operation Midnight Climax

The CIA, in the mid-sixties, wanted to study the concept and outcomes of LSD on students and civilians. The idea was that the agency wanted a leveraging study on drug trafficking, sex trafficking and the conduct of sexual abuses in the city of Los Angelo's and Washington. The agency would hire female prostitutes and they would send it would send the females to the rooms of drug lords. The prostitutes would contaminate the situations for the lords and gradually, compel them to spill the beans for drug trafficking. Here, dark psychology was passing with the concept of Dark Factor, where the agency, on the behest of its authority, wanted to have a command on the drug lords.

The Monster Study

This study was carried out by Dr. Wendell Johnson and Mary Tudor and they studied twenty-two children with imperfect care and zeal. They brought the children to their houses and created two group of children. One group was given positive speech notes and they were praised for their slight bit of contribution while speaking. The other group was a negative a speech note, where every word of the child, was belittled and defamed. The outcomes of this study were dark as well, because the children's mental cognition and behavioral practices never became as per the requirements of a sane individual and the research became very petrified about this. This Monster Study was never really published because of the fear that the researchers might get arrested of it.

Project MKUltra

From the year 1953 to 1973, the United States conducted a series of manipulating experiments for their citizens. The reason for such experiments were to induce, excessive drug use, the use of harsh words, emotional abuse, sexual abuse, psychological abuse and what not. The results became very hedonistic in their nature and ultimately the cases and subjects were meant to be shut down. The project MKUltra was halted by the Congress and in time, it was politically removed for the betterment of society.

The Aversion Project

This historical dark process was a landmark in Dark continuum. The apartheid era in South Africa was on its horizon and many people had to be displaced from their homelands seeking refugee in neighboring countries. The spree of homosexuality was prevalent in South Africa and they wanted to cure themselves in a therapist manner. Dr. Aubrey Levin was put in charge by the government of USA to cure the plight of the homosexuals. According to the doctor back then, the people of homosexuals were facing a mental disorder due to which, the homosexuals were unable to cure themselves. They started fleeing themselves away and doctor wanted to erase their sexual orientation by making them realize the harms of being a homosexual. The idea was that the homos must be displaced with nude pictures of gays and lesbians and they will be forced to curse them. Doing this, will make them unable to have any kind of love affiliation with any gay and they will feel all great and strong. Therefore, the aversion project was done on the sole purpose that how gays and lesbians are evil and bad in their utter character and quite possibly, this project can lead to success and sustenance.

Unnecessary Sexual Reassignment

Sexual Reassignment is a process, which tends to reassign and alter the sex of an individual through biological and scientific means. This process came to limelight when a nine-year-old boy's gender was reassigned as doctors were not sure of his apparent gender. His penis was circumcised during a mental process and with the passage of time, he had to be reassigned further. This trauma was a sever condition for the parents and they did not know what measures they need to adopt to finish this problem. They want to the doctors bashing their claims and the people had to face some observations regarding this matter as well. Therefore, this was a dark process, which was made to induce a horror spirit in the children of people so that they could remain an isolation in their approach.

Stanford Prison Experiment

This experiment was conducted in the midst of 1971, where prisoners and guard men were able to speak to one another and the people had to face the moral outcome of it. The idea was there needing to be the causes depiction between prisoners and guards and then their culture of interaction could be studied better. The people, who had been given the role of guard were taking their respective genres in a bad manner. The prisoners began to enforce harsh measures on the guards and the guards were not able to confess the suitability of that as well. The prisoners accepted the abuses in a rational manner and the people had to flee away from the cause by all means necessary.

Milgram Experiment

This experiment was conducted to understand the nature of Nazis, after the world war two. This Milgram experiment was designed to see if the patient is able to see the harsh realities of life and can be conform to the authority or not. There was a test tube that was placed on the sides of the patient and a questioning panel was placed in front of him. The panel asked some nefarious questions to him and made him realize that he was quite incompetent and could not able to answer good and subtle answers. This proved a dark mechanism in the minds of the people and the panel that psychology is very relevant in the scenario of people. Therefore, the Milgram experiment was a torturing way to express sorrow and sadness in the minds of people and hence, it was expunged off or halted by the people by all means necessary.

The Monkey Drug Trials

This event was an epitome of dark psychology in which animals were tested. They were injected with drugs and the outcomes of drugs were carefully examined by the public. The public rendered its advices to the people and made sure that how the reaction would lead the animals. This reaction was a necessary ingredient of the testing of animals and it was asserted in the means of people by all means necessary. The monkey trial gave a dark side of psychology to the public and with the passage of time, it was assured that monkeys are detriment to the society. Therefore, the monkey drug trials exhibited a darker version of the animals as well and people came to this result very quickly.

Facial Expressions Experiment

This experiment was conducted on the basis of studying the facial expression of people while providing them an external stimulus. In this experiment, it was asserted that people that have some mental troubling issues will be given an external stimulus so that the persons are able to have an impact of it. The facial expressions are there to judge the internal conditions of the individuals and then the personalities of the individuals are carefully assessed. The system is quite inherent in this manner and the people are able to give proper justification to the external responses. The external responses include the use of drugs, porn movies, the inducing of drugs and devastation and many more. The facial expression experiment gives the students and the clients a justification that the people are not able to have a sustainable present in them.

Little Albert

This was the dark hour of the psychological era. The founder of behaviorism, Mr. John Watson was deemed as the dark executor of this regime and he named some of the children to be equally liable in this regard. He would take a young child in his custody and he would test the abilities of him. Little baby Albert was exposed to many sounds and other stimulus, which made him feel quite bad and slurry. This was done to condition fear of little Albert and with the passage of time,

Albert was made quite inhumane in this regard. Therefore, little Albert had to be taught something great about the channeling of darkness and atrocity in the present and with the passage of time, dark psychology made this landmark achievement that psychology can also be used to condition fear and badness.

Bobo Doll Experiment

This experiment was conducted to see the violent learnt behavior of children. Seventy-five children were taken from the primary school and they were positioned in the market to get more and more insight about the dark nature of the children. Dr. Albert Bandura was the psychologist in the experiment and he was given a strong assurance of the child's psyche and the child needs to be given more and more creativity to the matter of the children. Bandura repeated the experiment twice in the reflection of the students and it seemed like the children did not like it as well.

The results were that the children were continuously affected by dark continuum and dark myths and they were made to resolve to the experiments in an effective manner.

The pit of Despair

The psychologist used in this tenure was an unethical professor, who would embark on the prospects of animal harshness. With the passage of time, the monkeys were given clinical depression results and at the coming time, there was a strong mode of cause and effect in the children. These were some of the young tests that were done to perform the characters of the animals and there was a mode of dark methods in them. The monkeys were made very starve and hectic while experimenting and it seemed like they were in a pit of despair.

The Bystander Effect

This effect was the checking of the mindsets of the people that witnessed murder at a near distance and did not do anything. This effect was based on the actual story and it was about Kitty Genovese, who was stabbed by thirteen people and the people that were watching her did not do anything. This is the idea that needs to be assessed here that people witnessing murder must not think of anything rather to simply help the victim or the person, who is in serious jeopardy. The subjects that were seen observing a murder state were not able to qualify for the stance of Kitty and this was made very pernicious in this regard. Therefore, the concept of dark psychology was strengthened in this experiment and people went very pugnacious in this matter.

Learned Helplessness Experiment

This experiment was taught on the conduct of dogs and there was a learned helplessness that was seen prevalent among the people. The public thought of learned helplessness as a disease that could be very harmful for the persons and in order to see the condition of the animals, dogs were given a state of helplessness. This state defined that the dogs were not able to respond effectively to the state of happiness and they would run away. Their running away asserted the slogan that people have to be treated in a proportional manner so that the public would be give enough lessons about harmony and strength. Thus, in order to diffuse the state of lawlessness and dark syndrome among the humans, this state of learned helplessness was achieved.

Racism among elementary schools

When Martin Luther Junior was assassinated, racism never really ended. People were still treated in a demonic manner and many still had to witness the downfall of humanity among themselves. The worst exhibition of racism can be seen in the midst of 80s, when the class room children were treated with the spree of racism. The black and white children were segregated in the class. The black people were not able to communicate with the people as pe teacher's instruction and every now and then, they were maliciously treated. This experiment was not conducted by a psychologist but a teacher did it just to imbue racism among the pupils. This culture of hatred was seen prevalent in the minds of teachers and with the passage of time, this ideology was sponsored by the state level as well. Hence, dark psychology was seen exhibited in the crux of racism among the children in the midst of 80s.

UCLA Schizophrenia Experiments

The Schizophrenia Experiments were conducted by CIA to know the adverse effects of Schizophrenia among the people so that the agency could carry on the study for a longer duration of time. It was believed by then that the people that are suffering from Schizophrenia are ill in their nature and they must be put to death. Almost forty people were used in this experiment and their mentalities were checked in order to see what are the results of the experiments. The idea is simple that people are ought to be checked in tough conditions and the people will come in cognizance of the battle that made them quite close to them. The Schizophrenia are the people that do not have mental incarnations among them but they have worse spree of characteristics that galore them. These experiments were tantamount to dark psychologist and the people are not able to transform the mindsets of the individuals in a better and longer way. Hence, dark psychology was clearly exhibited in this process with full zeal and courage.

The wild boy of Aveyron

Aveyron was a forest place in the dark woods of medieval era and in the late 1800s, the psychologist found a lost boy named anonymous. He was a feral lad, who was named victor by the psychologist. Victor was a perfect example of the case nurture versus nature. The aspects of nature were in him like wilderness, wildness and wideness of thoughts. However, the concepts of nurture were missing in him and there were people that wanted to induce a spirit of warmness and helpfulness in them. The idea here is the dark psychology tends to strengthen itself with the use of power and assertiveness and this is something that was carefully seen in this case study.

Therefore, these are some of the historical cases that see into the evolution of dark psychology in the past, present and future. The people wanted to see the prospects more carefully and assertively.

Manipulation Psychology

This chapter will carefully deal with the definition of manipulation psychology. This is the branch of psychology that deals with the aspects of Manipulation and hard work. Some of the signs of Manipulation are as follows:

The use of Home court

This is the manipulation technique in which the individual uses his or hers home as an advantage for his own benefits. The psychological demeanor was used to define the crux of the people, who were under the liability of the people. For the substantiation of this case, it is important to understand that the people, who are in a psychological condition to manipulate others are very smart. The first rule is that the public must come into consideration of the psychological master and then the master will navigate his thoughts. First and foremost, the master uses the court to manipulate the personalities and then the public first advocate the use of manipulation to be just and obscure.

Establishing the stance first and then looking for weaknesses

In the manipulation of psychology, it is important to understand that the establishment of the stance is first. The stance needs to be manifested first and then it is established so that the people, who are listening the track come under the way of the manipulator. Once the stance of the manipulator is established then the maneuvering is very easy. The people have to understand the use of the stance easily and then they have to use the words of the manipulator as a source of manipulation. The people can easily be thrown into abyss when the manipulator asks a lot of questions. The idea is that the public first navigates the stance and then the manipulator can use the stance to find its justification. If the manipulator wants to find the essence of the stance and if he finds some distortion of the stance then he can avoid the crux of the stance very badly.

Manipulation of Facts

If you want to assert the significance of the psychology of manipulation, then the facts stated can be used to deceived. The facts can be of any statement and that can be used to defy the logic of the people. For instance, if the manipulator is using the fact sound of one thing then that thing can be used to defy as well. Persons that can assess the logic of the personalities can manipulate by navigating them through their own lies. This is the act of manipulation if the people are using the effects of deviance in an effective manner.

Overwhelming with facts and statistics

First and foremost, the fact and statistics can be used to defy the personalities of the public. The facts are to be constructed in an effective manner so that the manipulator can be used to defy the odds of manipulation. So, for a strong manipulation, you have to overwhelm the facts and statistics with the persons. The persons can be used to come under the clout of statistics if the public are not able to use strong mode of psychological messages. Therefore, it is important that psychology can be used to interpret the essence of the public in a logical manner.

Overwhelming with procedures and Red tape

In order to maintain the crux of other personalities, the manipulator uses procedures and red tapes to give more defying reasons to the public. The manipulator will use the procedural versions, in which the public has to be manipulated in a stringent manner. The manipulator can be harnessed in a strong way so that the public can give concrete methods to it. For this reason, to be constructed, the manipulator uses some procedures and advantages through which the normal public comes into oppression. This oppression is used to defy the lands of the public and the public comes under the manipulation of the manipulator. So, in order to manipulate the people, the psychologists can use the crux of procedures and some secretive tapes that can be used in a strong manner.

Raising the voice and Displaying Negative Emotions

The manipulator in order to make the voice of the public effective has to raise the voice of himself. The manipulator uses some strong means and modes through which he is able to forecast a shadow of darkness. This darkness is used to construct the methods of manipulation among the stakeholders and the people can come under effective modes of destruction. Also, the negative emotions, give the value of harsh realities among the public and they get severely neglected by the personalities. Therefore, it is important to understand that the public are not able to get manipulated if they see the raised level of voice and hence there is a display of festering emotions among the people.

Negative Surprises

The negative surprises are another mode of manipulation by the manipulator. The manipulate can be using harsh negative surprises through which the people are not able to understand their nature. These negative surprises also affect the effects of mentality of the public and with the passage of time, the people do not get easily comfortable in this essence. The negative surprises show a strong moment of disinterest among the public and there is a culture of disassociation among the public through the negative surprises. The negative surprises give a sense of bad omens for the public through which the people are not able to give standard modes of deviation for the public.

Giving you a little or no time to decide

The time that has been given to you is either less time or there is no time. The manipulator wants to get his thing done because only then he is effective in his mode. The manipulator would cast his own means to come in front of the public. The time that has been slotted for the manipulator has a strong version of connectedness with the people and thus, there needs to be a strong sense of affection for the people. Therefore, the time of decision that has been given to you is a tool of the manipulator so that the public is able to give more directions for the public. So, the time has to be a motive interest for the public to understand in an effective manner.

Use of Negative Humor

The negative humor is a manipulating tool to disassociate you from your being. The manipulator would cast a negative humor on you and will do his best in making you feel bad about the situation. This manipulation is further designed by the manipulator to disempower you and with its continuous bolstering, the use of negative humor could be very harsh and brutal for you. Therefore, the use of negative humor could be used to induce isolationism and fanaticism in the public and could be very pernicious for you as well. If the use of negative humor could be bad for you then manipulation could be a stringent maneuver to showcase in-effectiveness among you.

Consistent Judgement

The consistent judgement could be a harsh tactic to induce fright among you. The manipulator could use the essence of judgement to make you feel discomfort able. How it can be done? This is as follows: Suppose, you are sitting in a room and the manipulator is sitting in front of you and you are able to hear the statements of the manipulator and with the passage of time, the public is not able to define the essence of the judgments properly. The public is quite effective in harboring the essence of the manipulator and if the manipulator is successful is dissing you with his judgements then finally you are under his claw. The consistent judgment will make you feel very demotivated and with the passage of time, you will be feeling delusional.

Silent Treatments

When the manipulator wants to harbor his mechanism then he uses the edifice of silence. This silence is very haunting. It is very managerial and with the passage of time, it induces a bad version of manipulation among you. You get affected by the silence of the manipulator and in time, this becomes very pestering among you. The silent treatment is also very haunting at an individualistic level because at times, the public are not able to see the results of it in a discomforting manner. Therefore, the silent treatments can be used to haunt the premises of the individual in a bad manner.

Pretend Ignorance

The manipulators can be used to see the edifice of ignorance in them. The people can be used to see the harmful effects of ignorance and the public can come into the direct affiliation of the manipulator. The manipulator could be seen pretending like he is ignoring the answers of the public but he is actually bolstering the acts of manipulation for the public. Therefore, it is important to understand that the public must cater to this regard seriously and if anyone is seen being ignorant then he/she is using manipulation. Thus, the idea is simple over here, if a person is able to see the harmful effects of ignorance in it then he can see what can actually lead in to it. Therefore, it is necessary to understand that pretension of ignorance is actually a mode to attain the prospects of ignorance.

Guilt-Baiting

There is a strong perception that the manipulators can easily use the edifice of guilt baiting in them. This is the idea that makes the manipulator plays the victim card. The manipulator aims himself to be the victim caretaker and with the passage of time, he starts to play the victim card with full zeal. The idea is that the more victimhood the person has to play, the more he gets into wrong and unnecessary means and progression. Also, with the victim card, the public has to see what are the harms and ills of the people, therefore, it is important to understand that the manipulator can be used in some essence of the presence of the public to disapprove any of its matter.

Victimhood

There are some of the imaginal victim hood believes in the minds of the manipulator that make him believe that he is the actual victim. He gets so strangled by the cost of doing bad things, that he focuses himself to be totally bad and pugnacious. All these believes make the manipulator believe that he has been severe victim of the public and with the passage of time, the victim has to be addressed with empathy and sympathy. The sympathy starts with this belief that the people are able to have a great amount of interest for the public and the people.

Therefore, the culture of victimhood is a mode of making the person feel empowered by self-asserting himself to be a victim.

So, these are some of the manipulation techniques used in psychology to deceive the personalities in the future.

Manipulator's Tools

This chapter will precisely deal with the tools and tactics that are used by a manipulator to imbue the methods of manipulation. Those can be the clever words of language, use of cultural norms and the societal inclination among the public. It can be many other things as well.

Ten tools and Techniques used by the Manipulator

Following are some of the techniques

1. Gaslighting

This is the technique that is used to see if the person's words sound like his actions or not. The gaslighting is a method that can be used to question the belief of the personality and with the passage of time, the person has to understand the use of this tool to use the manipulation effectively. There is a set of questions among the public, used by the manipulator to dodge the essence of the questions and with the passage of time, the entire scenario of the public changes with time all because of the gas questions, asked by the manipulator.

2. Generalizations

The generalizations of a manipulator are a strong sense of demotivation for the public to withstand. The manipulator easily generalizes all the terms and tactics that are employed on a social, economic and political factor and with the passage of time, the generalizations come with time. The generalizations are important enough for a manipulator for the student to understand the essence of all compatible reasons for the public and with the passage of time, the manipulator is able to see the distance of the public go far away. Therefore, the distance of the public from the real cause actually defines the status of the manipulator and with the manipulator can control a lot of sense through it. Therefore, the use of a generalizing matter creates more and more aspect for the students and civilians. Thus, the use of generalization gives impetus to the manipulator and with the passage of time, it can be more asserted in the coming. So, generalization can lead to a lot of trouble and menace for the student.

3. Moving the goal post

The manipulators have every right to deny your goal and ambition. They call it the moving of goal post and this is how the public is able induce bad and obscene mechanism to it. The goal post is the ambition of every man to cater to the fundamentally obsessed question of the incident and with the passage of time, the manipulator tends to de-track you from the quest at the earliest. The track is therefore a sense of motivation for you and you do not get enough style of aspiration for the students and civilians. The idea is quite simple that the public are able to create more satisfaction for the public and with the passage of time, the manipulators induce havoc as well.

4. Changing the subject

The manipulator would do his best in changing the subject. This aspect makes avoid accountability of his previous actions and with the passage of time, he learns the act of treachery and deception. Any time or anyplace, where he is not able to see the masterpiece of the subject, he tends to foil with the public and therefore, he is not even governing to the matter of the public so that he could not even to the matter of appreciation. Thus, changing the subject of any conversation is also a tool of manipulation that is required by all means necessary.

5. Name-calling

Name-calling is an art and tactic that can be used to induce marginalization in the incident and with the passage of time, it could lead to dilemmas and destruction. The name calling starts with a mode of aspiration for the pupils but ends in utter destruction for the public. This concept can be easily seen in many areas and portions of the world and such a practice can induce horror and terror in the region. This practice of name calling can be used in the factors that enable one with destruction and devastation.

6. Smear Campaigns

This campaign is used to address the horrendous use of psychology for the public. This is a play in which you are the victim and they are the martyr. According to them, you have displayed a sense of bad relationship to them and for that mere reason they have labeled you as a dead person. You no longer have a sense of reputation in the system and every time you encounter them, they tend to call you bad and the gone one. This aspect has many difficulties for you and end up being a psychopath. This aspect has emotional issues for you, psychological issues for you, ovulational and many more. Therefore, smear campaigns are personally made to make you feel bad and obscene and with the passage of time, you feel very hectic.

7. Devaluation

This devaluation is not the currency devaluation but it is the human devaluation of yourself, you tend to be very bad and obsolete in your character that you embarrass every one's exes. You will as it is your pertinent duty to make the lives and ages of others feel embarrassing and with the passage of time, you control over your anger just to inflict punishment among the others. For instance, there was a time when people were able to cooperate with one another and could not try to defame others. However, with the burgeoning social media, people tend to decide the relationship of others by making them feel very degenerate. This is the crucial aspect of psychology, which could be very tumultuous for you and with the passage of time, he felt very bad and worse. Therefore, devaluation is meant to be an outlet of dark psychology and it can be very harmful for anyone, who does it.

8. Aggressive Jokes

Aggressive Jokes are the modes to make others look small and in shambles. These jokes could be of anything like the jokes on individuality, the jokes on society and the jokes on caste. These jokes impose derogatory remarks on the individuals and with the passage of time, the individuals feel very bad about them. The idea is simple that the psychology believes that manipulators could be worst nightmares for innocent personalities. People can use the edifice of others to personally sabotage the concept of friendliness and equality among the persons and with the passage of time, the people tend to showcase a system of defamation among others. Thus, aggressive jokes can be bad and hazardous for others.

9. Triangulation

This is the concept, in which the individuals tend to use the supposed threat of others to manipulate the innocents. Suppose there are three individuals in a room, two of them are having an argument about anything and the person sitting next to them is of a high caste. The manipulator would use the edifice of supposed threat of the third person to deter that of a second person and with the passage of time, the concept of triangulation would be bolstered. Hence, the use of force and manipulation is done in order to make the third parties very bad and degenerate.

10.   Use of tools

In this paragraph, the tools that can be used for manipulation will be discussed. These are sensory devices, visual sensor, automatic assembly, industrial manipulator and photoelectric detector. These tools cast a shadow of degeneration among the personalities and with the passage of time, the people are able to have list of traumata embedded in them. Therefore, with the passage of time the tools can be used for a stringent version of collaboration.

Thus, these are some of the ways and tools of manipulation that can harbor bad deeds in the person.

How to recognize a manipulator

This chapter will clearly look into this concept that how the manipulator can be interpreted and how it can be recognized. This will help you to stay from the manipulator as long as you require.

Warning signs of a manipulator

The warning signs of a manipulator are as follows:

1. He is charming and nice

The manipulator is all charm and nice at first. He would try his best in making you feel comfortable and gradually, he would impart his shrewdness. First, he would come in your comfort zone by wishing you birthdays, by giving you gifts and making you feel less agitated about anything then he would cast his dogmas. Once he knows that you will not bother him about anything then he would tell you to do anything by all means necessary. Sometimes, his manipulation is so strong and stringent that he can make you do anything even a murder. Thus, this is the idea of manipulation that is started with charming voices and ending in catastrophe. Beware of such people.

2. Denial

The manipulator would always deny any assertion or statement of guilty on him. He would be felt exempt of any charges and would dare to see himself in the crux of any problem. If you somehow even manage to bring him in any disaster then he would just simply run away and would assert his innocence over charges. He would think of himself as a strong mode of eccentricity and he would deny any kind of charges on him and would plead his innocence all over time.

This is the true nature of denial that it tends to be very compulsive and bad in its progression and becomes haunting as well. Therefore, the denial is able to make the people look very bad and obsolete to the individual.

3. Lying

The people are able to lie a lot and those, who can actually conform themselves on it are lying. The lying edifice starts with the inculcation of hate speech and derogation and with the passage of time, the people tend to learn a lot of lying. The innocents are not able to see the manifestation of lying in their inner sides and they do not how exactly is the platform of lying quite degenerate about it. The lying helps the manipulator to learn more and more about the advances of the individual and with the passage of time, he comes one step closer tin dodging and abhorring you. This is the strong crux of lying that needs to be strengthened by all means necessary.

4. Excessive Flattery

This sign is of huge importance with the manipulator. The manipulator is able to do a lot of flattery for the individuals and with the passage of time, the individual can harbor flattery and sweetness among the individuals. The flattery helps to manipulate the individuals in a strong manner and this flattery can be of any side and sustenance. The idea exhibited here is quite strong as the people are able to create an environment of justice and order in the citizens and the flattery helps to regulate themselves in an effective manner.

5. Forced Teaming

The individual can use the teaming of the layers for his own motives. This teaming can be devious in its nature and can reflect many ills and whims of the societies. The teaming can also lead to a social segregation in the society and with the passage of time, the person can easily regulate its crux in a mature manner. The force teaming can appoint strong versions of impact for the students and with the passage of time, the individuals can come up with strong assertions. The forced teaming could be the use of any strength and value and it could be very destructive in its nature as well. Therefore, forced teaming is a sign of affection for the manipulator and it is destruction for the students as well.

6. Good First Impression

The manipulator will always do his best in making the best impression that he can in order to carefully influence the minds of other people. This is a well-managed task just to make sure that the audience is under the reflection of the manipulator and you will all means necessary, follow under the trap of the manipulators. The good impression can be very expressive in its command and it can yield to proper potential as well but its lasting impacts are very pernicious. With the subtle use of good impression, the person can easily establish his core links with you and can make you do almost everything. Therefore, a person having an expression of good impression in him will be interpreted as a manipulator.

7. Pretending to be a victim

The manipulator is of a harsh and smart demeanor. He knows that of he will pretend to be a victim then all the persons will listen to him and no matter what are the conditions his stance and statements will stand correct. He will understand this assertion in a jiffy and will do his best in making the public very bad and obscene. The idea is simple that the person is not able to convey his true propositions to the public and he pretends to be a victim. The concept of victimhood tarnishes his image and with the passage of time, he tends to deviate from the straight path. This mere concept completely obstructs the use of empathy from the manipulator's mind and with the passage of time, he feels very degenerative. Therefore, the person, who is a manipulator, will always have sign of victimhood in him.

8. Silent Treatment

This sign is of strong admiration in the person, who is playing to be a manipulator. The manipulator will easily treat the level of punishment to the audience and while doing this, he will be silent and stringent as hell. This is the idea of concealing and secrecy that the manipulator employees and with the passage of time, he is able to impart a devious mechanism of dealing thing upon the individual. Therefore, it is important to observe the silent treatment of things in the public, and this silent treatment will actually make the person feel very atrocious. Therefore, in order to see the sign of manipulation the person has to be very silent and if he is found silent then yes, he is a manipulator.

9. Appearing to be selfless

The signs of selflessness are the signs that make the individual look very harsh and strong. The selflessness comes in the individuals either he has a golden heart or is he using the emblem of selflessness for himself. For instance, a boy, who is a manipulator falls in love for a person and asserts her to be selfless. In the moment, perhaps he is vouching for a love affair but in true sense, he tends to be manipulative. He would cast the shadow of badness upon the girl just to have an advantage of her and even get something from her. Therefore, the use of selflessness is also a quality that needs to be strengthened properly.

10.   Guilt Tripping

The idea of guilt-tripping is essential to understand as to decipher the nature of manipulation. In the guilt-tripping, the manipulator harbors the power of guilt in an individual and with the passage of time, he manipulates the other individual uses his guilt. He showcases that he is no the one, who is guilt and he trips the momentary aspects of guilt just to convey his innocence. This is a culture of guilt-tripping and it is easily found in all the corners of the world. Even international leaders use the edifice of guilt-tripping to transcend a culture of guilt-tripping. Therefore, it is important to understand that guilt-tripping can lead to a devastating blow of injuries and badness.

11.   Shaming

When the manipulator easily acquires his motives, he starts shaming others. He feels that individual is of no worthy and in order to destroy him completely, he must be shamed. He would shame you using harsh means, he would kill you possibly, he would employ derogatory remarks upon you and he would instill a culture of deviance among you. Therefore, the culture of shaming is found prevalent among the manipulators and if one has to recognize a manipulator, then he can use this edifice for good reasons. This is the revering identity of the individuals by all means necessary.

12.   Intimidation

The person is able to intimidate the other personality if he is manipulative. The manipulation is a hectic task as it requires a lot of effort for the manipulator to intimidate you. This intimidation can be strong as it could lead to an effective mode of manipulation for the individuals. The intimidation starts with a turning point as it will create more efflux of opportunities for the personalities for you. This culture of intimidation is great as you can create more manipulative tactics for your self but in the end, it will be harsh for you. Therefore, it is mandatory to understand that intimidation is a recognizing aspect of a manipulator.

13.   Diversio

Diversio refers to the diversity of opinion among the manipulators so that the people can easily lead to a better productive scenario of people to people contact. This diversity is important for you as it will yield greater sense of affection for you and in the presence of time, you will be able to diversify your opinion based on a common strand of diversity. This means that the manipulator can use the edifice of diversity just to yield more manipulation and strength in him. This can be taken in the aspect of plurality of opinion and in many ways, it can be dangerous as well.

Therefore, these are some of the ways and maneuvers through which the manipulator tends to manipulate and impact you with dark psychology. It is your duty to see if the person can be easily affected by it or not.

Techniques of dark persuasion, mind control, dark seduction

In this chapter, the techniques of dark persuasion, mind control and dark seduction will be examined. All of the three concepts can be started earlier and move on with the progression as well. Therefore, the illustration is as follows:

Techniques of Dark Persuasion

Following are some of the dark techniques for dark persuasion.

1. Foot in the door

The foot in the door means that you are asking for a small favor first and then you ask for a dark favor. This is the favor that could be very effective for you and in term can lead to a bad and obscene prospect. The manipulator would first use the aspect of manipulation so that the people would listen to the manipulator and then the manipulator would charge his nutshells among the people. This is a devious terminology, which is designed to give more and more agitation to the public.

2. Door in the face

For this technique to b effectively implemented, it is important for the manipulator to ask something, which is quite easy and effective for you. The door in the face means that you ask for something very subtle and you tend be affectionate in its manner. The asking is of polite and it is something, which is easily accessible by the persons, but with the passage of time, the offer gets more invitation and you tend to disagree with it. Therefore, this offer is a gateway for the manipulator to have his ends meet.

3. Anchoring

Anchoring helps you to give leverage on many problems and the manipulator can easily use it to display a sense of affection for the public. The affection starts with an offer and then the manipulator fulfills to price required to do the job. This pricing is a gateway for the personalities to understand the essence of anchoring and the people, get to know the essence of manipulation in easier manner. This anchoring can also be interpreted as pricing and once the manipulator fulfills the ideologies of anchoring then the person gets the idea in an effective manner.

4. Commitment and Consistency

The commitment and consistency are a gateway for the manipulator to get to know the advancements of issues and with the passage of time, he also fulfills them. The commitment and consistency are necessary for the manipulator to harbor and with the passage of time, the people are able to distill the level of trust with the manipulator. The manipulation is an important mode of affection for the people and thus, with the passage of time, the manipulator gets to know the advancements in a better manner.

5. Social Proof

This is a smart persuading technique, in which the person uses the social proof and it maintains a link of affection for the other people. The manipulator easily creates a sense of ideological confrontation for the persons and the persons can get a large sense of commitment through it. This means that there is a disembarking of an idea that is followed by all and by strong assertion, the person is able to have a strong moment of content for the persons. Therefore, with the passage of time, the person is able to have a strong social proof in the coming time.

6. Authority

For persuading anyone, it is vital that the manipulator holds authority in his hand. The use of force and the compelling nature of the manipulator will serve his interest in a better manner and together, the manipulator is able to cast a great shadow of maneuvering among the people. Thus, the authority rests in the house of officials and the manipulator and this technique can be used in many of the forms efficiently. Authority commands dignity.

7. Scarcity of Resources

Manipulators try to market their assertions in a common manner. They will show as something is unavailable in the market and will showcase its assertions in a common manner. With the passage of time, the scarcity is carefully ensured by the marketer of the individual and he is not able to formulate better postures of it. He shows as if he has the authority of all the commands but the scarcity of the resources is a way to dodge the loyalty of other personalities. Therefore, the scarcity of resources is a method to employ good means of manipulation for the students and the pupils as well. Therefore, it is essential to understand the nature of manipulation and regardless of any issues, the scarcity is an endeavor to boost manipulation among the manipulator.

8. Reciprocation

Reciprocation is a method to persuade as well. When times the individuals are able to harbor the context of reciprocation, they channel the crux of reciprocation. Many a times, the individuals are not able to reciprocate the concept of affiliation and they want to unnecessarily reciprocate. This reciprocation is done to show that how the people are able to transform their lives and they have the pertinence of other individuals as well. Many times, the individual has done something for the public and the public does not want any reciprocation but still there is reciprocation.

These were the techniques of dark persuasion and now the techniques of mind control will be discussed in brevity.

Techniques of Mind Control

The techniques are as follows:

1. Do all the thinking

The manipulators will do their best in doing the thinking for you. They will think for you and will tell you the best for you. However, the doing revolves around the crux of manipulation. They are doing this so that you can be in their domain and thus, there mind control tactic is successful. This is the better prospect for you and once you do this, you are in the action of the mind control.

2. Starting an avalanche

The avalanche is a marketing firm that makes you strong and subtle in their regard. The creation of an avalanche is pertinent for you to understand and with the passage of time, there is a secret maneuvering for you and you will induce an avalanche for you. The avalanche for you is that you have to be in the claws of an avalanche for you. Therefore, the mindset of the individual is easily dodging and with the passage of time, he is able to have a control of the manipulator.

3. Ask for an inch take a mile

The asking for an inch and taking a mile is a concept that asserts the importance of taking things quickly. This means that the manipulator would cast a shadow quickly and with the passage of time, he would ask things for you which would have no actual reasons. This can be explained with an example. The manipulator would do a big favor for you and in return, you would love to comply him and with the passage of time, the manipulator would not take your compliments. He would ask of something great and then he would take a profuse amount. This is the basic tenant of manipulation that ask something else and get all-in return.

4. Always have real deadline

The real deadline means that the person has to realistically forecast a shadow line on you and you are not expected to do anything in return. The deadline means that you will do something for him and in return, he will give you proper isolation for you. Therefore, it is important to understand the nature of you and you will have the prospects in no time. The real deadline refers to the last concept of the material and with the passage of time, you will get a new result in the formation.

5. Giving ten times more

The manipulator will be able to leverage himself by giving you more and more things. If he does something for you and in return you do better for him. Then this is the mode of affection for him. Therefore, the giving of ten-time will provide you a sustainable moment of affection for yourself. This is exactly the method of utilization for you and you will be able to have more relaxation of it. Therefore, the giving of more things is actually a way to control the minds of the public and he will get more and more insight of it. Thus, the giving of more and more things will provide you with better affection.

6. Standing for something greater for you

The people are able to get in your mind control if they believe in you. In order for them to believe in you, you have to do something great for them. To an extent, that they will always recall of you while they are pursuing something and they are able to have a problem in any situation. In this way, they will harbor all the mechanisms for you that will induce a great sense of affection for you. Therefore, the standing for something is actually an act of affection for you and the people around.

7. Be shameless

The people are always shameless, who want to manipulate you carefully. They feel as it is their importance to have you onboard for their progression. They believe that the people will understand you effectively if they are shameless. Being shameless does not mean that they dance in all nudity for you but in actual terms, they are able to have a strong sense of affection for you. Therefore, being shameless is an attribute to you so that you are able to have a precautionary sense of affection in you.

Techniques of Dark Seduction

There are some rules and tactics to be used in the era of dark seduction.

1. Eye seduction

In psychology, you can use the edifice of eye to eye connection in order to make the eyes look greater and more effective. The eye effect is important to seduce the other end of personalities. The personalities are able to have a great sense of seduction in them due to which the public is able to have fun and persuasion. The eye seduction is tantamount to give more and more value to the psychologists and in time, they are able to have more fun and zeal in the eye seduction. Thus, it is important to do eye seduction in the coming time.

2. Using the lack nesses

In dark psychology, you can use the lack nesses of other personalities so that you can have the leverage on other personalities. You will understand in time that the individuals will be able to have more and more zeal in them. The lack nesses can give you more aspect in their clout. The clout can be more incisive in their regard. The use of edifice can help you give more and more aspiration in the coming. The psychologist and the manipulator will use this prospect to gain leverage in the coming time.

Therefore, these are some of the techniques that can be used to have more entertainment in their regard. Also, the concept is brighter and more effective in their mechanism.

The characteristics of an easily manipulated person

This chapter will look incisively into the details of the manipulated person. The manipulated person is the one that gets prone to manipulation and can have a greater version of affection in them as well.

Traits of manipulated persons

The traits of a manipulated persons are as follows.

1. They are very innocent

Innocence describes the value of the manipulated person. They are emotionally ill and broken. They do not know what to do and what not to and they get easily affected by their assertions. They tend to be all-knowing and encompassing but in entirety, they are not able to cater to the best of all beings. In other words, they are so pugnacious in their beings and degenerations that they become clearly horrendous. In order words, they are the one, who are easily predated

2. They are looking for trust.

The manipulative person can cast all types of shadows on the individuals but the manipulated person is the one that is looking for trust. He feels that the individuals do not know the concept of trust and affection for the individuals and with the passage of time, the people are not able to get a better picture of the story. Therefore, the manipulated personality is looking for trust but, in the end, he is feeling very bad and obscene. Thus, it is important for us that we get away from all the devious manipulation for us in the coming time.

How to know you are a victim of manipulation

This chapter will delve into this thesis that the how to know that you are a victim of manipulation. Following are some of the signs.

1. Plain Old bullying

If your partner or any individual in the relationship is trying to bully you, then you are being the manipulated. The result of the manipulation will come late but the present bullying is the result that will make you go restless and repugnant to conciliation. You will feel that your entire life is in devastation and with the passage of time, you will tend to be more and more exhaustive. Thus, the concept of plain old bullying will be a hallmark of affection for you and you will feel very agitated in its regard.

2. Home Court Advantage

In any manipulation, the victim can understand its victimhood if the person is playing his home court advantage. This means that the person is not able to see the charms of life in a pleasant manner and he is feeling all bad and bodacious about it. The home court advantage makes him go restless and in the passage of time, the manipulation gets stronger. Thus, the use of home court advantage is a reflection of manipulation.

3. If you really cared about me

This technique grants a skeptic though to the manipulator that in order to make him more and more compulsive, he starts to ask more questions like if you had really cared about me and made me feel very great. If you had made me not so uncomfortable in the past and like how you can necessarily give more weightage in this regard. The idea to this method is one has to be very relaxed in the confession and keeps on avoiding any such statements, which can make him more and more instrumental in this regard.

4. Emotionally Blackmail

The emotional blackmailing is an aspect, which will have a lot of confusions for you in the coming. It will make you feel more and more inspirational in the coming and hence, you will be able to have a sound connection of emotions with you. The emotional blackmailing, if it is present then it can make the wills look bad and in times, it can make thing go in an effective manner. Therefore, the emotionally blackmailing is an aspect of manipulation and if it is prevalent in your relationship then you are being manipulated to a large extent.

5. Convenient Neediness

This neediness is the method, which is only done on convenience for the people. The manipulators will be using the convenient card to make the people be aware of the masses of the public and with the respect of time, it is mandatory for the people to get to the affection in a certain manner. The convenience helps the manipulators to help the message of their utility go in a start manner. Therefore, if you want to have a convenient bases of neediness in you then you can actually help others to achieve the best possible way possible.

6. Killing them with kindness

The kindness helps the individuals to know about the surface of the individuals. The manipulators use the edifice of kindness in a perpetual manner. The people will tend to look into the matter of others by possibly making them a culprit of their kindness and thus, the individuals can look into the regard in a possible manner. They manipulators would kill their relationships in a continuous way and hence, the people will come to know the edifice of kindness in a fair manner. Therefore, killing them with kindness will make the pupil know more and more about the just policies effectively. Hence, the killing aspect makes the kind gestures more productive and potential.

7. Very calm at the starting

The students tend to be very calm about the people all in the making. They make the individual more kind in their collection and the individuals make the aspect of kindness in a just manner. Therefore, the manipulators will be kind to you and if you want to make the best of the process. Try your best in making them manipulators go away.

All these tactics are the reasons why the manipulators are successful in manipulating others.

How to behave with a manipulator

The chapter will delve into the possibility that how to behave with the manipulator and what needs to be done in order to be at a distance with the manipulator. Following are some of the ways to outsmart a manipulator.

1. Avoid contact with the manipulator

First and foremost, do your best in avoiding contact with the manipulator. This means that the manipulator has to be firm and fervent in this regard and you have to do your best in befriending them. You can also make the contact look very dismissal and there is no need for you to be socially devoid of them.

2. Say no to being manipulated

You must not come in trust with manipulation. If there is a friend of you that is trying his best to manipulate him and then you must say no and must try your best in making the assertions look very bad. So that the individuals are able to make the stand at a far distance and you are not able make an assertion.

3. Ignore the words would be

Often the manipulator uses the words would be. You need to avoid and must never the listener build the case on it. The idea is simple that do not build any such statements and assertions that could be harmful for you. Therefore, you must do your best in ignoring the words would be and never let any issue try to harm or dismantle you. Therefore, the ignorance is important for you to understand so that you can yield a good life.

4. Always set personal boundaries

Never allow the manipulator to be at your personal side. Always set some personal boundaries, which will make you look very bad and obscene. Try your best in setting the personal boundaries of the people and make yourself look smart and stringent. Thus, the idea of setting personal boundaries will make you feel very confident and compound.

5. Set goals and tell others to be away with them

The idea of setting goals will make you understand that you have a vision and an aim in life. The setting of goals will make the manipulator go away and he will not bother you no matter what. The idea starts with a potent moment of consideration and with the passage of time, it is important for you to refrain from any indulgence and incarceration. The setting of goals will help the manipulator to go away and the person will be able to have a lot of fun for himself.

6. Stay calm

Whenever you talk with a manipulator, you will notice that they will try to overcome your passion with respect to time. You have to stay calm and will be if you are able to create more strong versions of time. The idea of staying calm will make you fall apart from the manipulator and you will be at the epitome of your life with concentration.

7. Say no firmly

If there is a job from the manipulator and he tends to disarray you then you have to say no. No can be in words and in actions as well and can personally, make you feel very great. You will be able to leverage the personality maker and with the passage of time, you will see that the persons are able to have a sound knowledge of it as well. The manipulator, who is doing this thing will make you feel very robust and within times, you will get to know the aspects of it in a better way. So, say no to the individuals and with the passage of time, you will feel very great and effective.

8. Assert yourself and be hard

Assertion is a hard tactic for the manipulator to handle. The manipulation can be forsaken with anything and with the passage of time, the assertion can help you make more comfortable and relaxing in time. The assertion is a necessary thing as well and it can lead to a better personality as well. Therefore, the assertion needs to be commanded with full zeal and courage.

9. Practice self-care

Always practice self-care, no matter what happens. You will understand that what is momentarily required to dodge a manipulator. The practice of self-care will make you feel very bad and with the respect of time, you will tend to be very strong and stringent. The idea is simple that you have to be very cohesive in your regard. The assertion is simple that one can lead to the prosperity of the question in a better way. The practice of self-care would be effective. Therefore, it is essential for you to understand the importance of self-care with full zeal and honor.

Therefore, these are some of the ways and mechanisms to make the behaving with the manipulator sound great.

The basics of brainwashing

In this chapter, the basics of brainwashing are important for the users to understand effectively and with the passage of time, the manipulator uses these basics to make the strangle of the manipulation more effective. The basics are as follows:

1. Isolation

Isolation starts with the basics of brainwashing. The brainwashing is important to understand by the manipulator. The manipulator would use the edifice of isolation. The isolation is effective in its use and by all means necessary, the manipulator tends to isolate you from social order. He makes you understand that the world is not effective in its use and can be very haunting in its meaning. Therefore, isolation is a technique used to be understood effectively.

2. Attacks on self-esteem

While brainwashing, the manipulator uses the edifice of attacks on self-esteem. For him, the brain of you is of high importance. Whatever he thinks of you can be altered only if he wishes to change your brain. You will make the self-esteem of yourself and by the prospects you will understand that the manipulator is using this edifice to brainwash you.

3. Mental abuse

In order for the brain washing to work more effectively, the use of mental abuse is of high importance. The use of mental abuse will work in a practical manner and will thwart the conformity of the brain precisely. The mental abuse can be used of mentality and effectively and with the passage of time, you will understand that you are seeking to feel very obscene. Therefore, the crux of mental abuse will be effective for you in its making.

4. Physical abuse

The physical abuse will look into the brainwashing in a complete manner. Do your best in avoiding the physical abuse of the manipulators. Otherwise, you will find yourself in a turbulent manner. The physical abuse can lead to the tarnishing of the brain and you will feel very bad at the end. Therefore, the concept of physical abuse must never be allowed to be furnished at the first place.

5. Only allowing contact with selected members

Brainwashers or manipulators want you to contact with selected members. The selected members will cater to the brainwashing effectively and with the passage of time, they can be successful if you do not object them at the first place. The selected members will showcase a culture of degeneration among you and with the passage of time, you will feel very bad and bodacious. Therefore, the contact hearing is only important for you if you wish to understand the nature of the selected members.

6. Us versus them

This slogan will make you understand that the entire slogan of unity will forever haunt you. The brainwashing gets its momentum when it is trending at a larger scale and there is a policy of us contamination with the them syndrome. This means that the US is not able to engage the them processors and with the passage of time, the people are able to have a strong fan page about it. Therefore, brainwashing is a tactic that is ensured in all better way to make the people look more and more great.

Hypnosis

This chapter will discuss the idea of Hypnosis and its role in psychology.

Hypnosis is a process, in which the individual responds to the stimulus of the questioner. The idea here is to test the mental ability of the persons in a gradual manner.

How does the hypnosis work?

This is the process, in which the psychologist is able to impact the role of tutor upon the coach. The idea is simple that the psychologists is of no more value to it and with the passage of time, the psychologist will govern the effects of the patient with respect to time. The idea is simple that the hypnosis needs to be worked in an effective manner and thus, the hypnosis will work effectively.

The effects of hypnosis can be very different to different to different individuals. Some individuals have a strong version of interest for the people while the others have a taste of disruption for others. The idea is simple that the effects can lead to a large extend of people for them and therefore, the people are able to make lesser version of interaction for others. Therefore, it is important to understand the hypnotic process is very subjective in its nature.

Hypnosis is used for the following purposes.

Purposes of use of Hypnosis

These are used as

1. Treatment of chronic pain conditions
2. Treatment of reduction of pain while child is happening
3. Reduction of Symptom of Dementia
4. Hypnotherapy may be helpful for certain symptoms

5. Reduction of nausea and vomiting conditions in time

6. Control of pain during dental positions

7. Elimination of reduction of pain during warts

8. Alleviation of symptoms

These are some of the purposes that can be very effective in their zeal and affection. There are many chances for the common individual to be addressed and affected by hypnotics. The children, the people and the elderly group can be easily affected by hypnosis.

The art of deception

Deception is a common thread in the dark psychology study. Deception can be done in various ways depending on the nature of the manipulator and the narcissist. Following are some of the ways of deceiving someone.

The ways to deceive some one

Following are some of the ways to deceive someone with full zeal.

1. Lie less and do more

The deceiving personality knows that he has to make sure of his conversations. If he lies more and more then he will get under the curve of badness and with the passage of time, he will feel himself to be bad. Also, there is a chance of him to get caught and could end himself in a bad manner. Therefore, in deception, the manipulator lies less and less and gets away from it.

2. Telling the truth in a misleading manner

Telling the truth in a misleading manner means that one has to be very effective in its regard. The telling of truth in a misleading manner showcases the strength of personalities and hence, the people are able to be maneuvered in a better way. Therefore, the deceiving personality uses the edifice of deception to make sure that the individual is all bad and worse in the frame.

3. The deceiver knows his target

The deceiver always does his best in knowing the target in an effective manner and when he approaches in an acute way, he tends to be very effective and efficacious in its rating. Therefore, the use of deception is a tool to know the target effectively and the time taken for its progress will also be used in a longer way.

4. Keep your facts straight

The keeping of facts straight makes you understand that what are the uses of fact measures. The idea is simple that the deceiving personality uses the facts straight and effective in its regard and with the passage of time, the facts are quite pertinent in its regard. Therefore, the keeping of facts means that the person is able to have a strong version of manipulation in him.

5. Staying Focused

The idea of staying focused is that the art of deception requires stealth and help. The stealth requires strong focus and assertion and with the passage of time, the man has to be very strong and sturdy in its manner. The focus paradigm will come in its manner and hence, the person is able to have a cure function of its people.

6. Watch your signals

The people are able to have a strong set of affection for themselves. The idea is simple that the deceiving personality will focus on the coming signals and with the passage of time, the personality will do its best in making the game more astute and effective. Therefore, the idea is simple for the psychologist and the manipulator to handle.

7. Always turn up the pressure

The turning up the pressure will always make the people look more and more agile. The pressure come with a stringent mode of affection and with the passage of time, the manipulator makes it look easier and more effective. Therefore, the use of pressure can ease the process in a curbing manner and thus, the deception will make the process more and more great.

8. Counter Attack

The personality uses the emblem of counter attack in order to make the deception effective. The menace used in this is that the deceiving personality uses the structure of counter attack and with the passage of time, there is a strong version of intellect for the people. The idea is simple and straight for the persons to come across and hence, the people are able to make more and more justice to this. The process starts with a better place to handle and therefore, the use of counter attack will make the things go way beyond the boundaries.

Therefore, these are ways to be used in the deception in a better way.

The dark triad. What it is and can be applied

Dark triad

The dark triad is the personality triangulation of narcissism, Machiavellianism and psychopathy. These triads can be helpful for the people to understand the crux of deception. The deception is harbored more effectively so that the personalities are able to induce conflict, the dilemmas and the use of agony for the people. The idea is simple that it can be applied for many uses as well.

The dark triad can be used in grandiosities, pride, egotism, manipulation, impulsivity, social disorders and remorselessness.

This can be applied in various levels. On an individual level, the dark triad can be applied in a better way so that the person is able to imbue affection and satisfaction in it. On a societal level, it can be used to harbor materialism and narcissism in them and on a political level, it can be used to make the things go way more effective and cordial in its manner. However, this dark triad can be made very haunting in its dimensions if the field is not able to be casted in a longer run. Therefore, the dark triad can help the narcissist to progress them in a subtle manner.

Case studies, famous examples

Following are some of the case studies employed in this regard for the chapter.

Freud's interest in Young Woman

This was the experiment that was conducted on the behest of Freud's relations with young women. In his Dark continuum, Freud believed that women, who do excessive masturbation are designed to be bad in nature and this is an ill-coordinated exercise that needs to be stopped. His experiments were many young women and out of them, was a young lady named, Emma. Emma had the problems with anxiety and depression and she used to do a lot of masturbation just to make the pain go away and ace the mental trauma. She decided that she will never ever dare to pursue a relationship and in order to ace herself, she went for a doctor, who happened to be Freud. Freud made her inhale serious nostril drugs, which made her go dizzy and how was she treated, remained a mystery for long. The concept of dark singularity can be seen in these experiments, where Freud is testing the enduring skills of Emma and wants to carry on the experiment at the cost of every result.

Electroshock Therapy on Children

Dr. Lauretta Bender of the Creedmoor Hospital believed that children, who do not have any social order in their characters are prone to be tested under an electroshock machine. She would invite many students to her lab and would not see the problems of the children clearly rather would ask some tough questions that would draw children towards confusion. When the children won't be able to answer it then she would put them under an electroshock computer and with the passage of time, the children would lose their subconsciousness and be paranoid. This aspect, according to Dr. Lauretta was a tool to make the children active and strong but, in its progression, the experiments proved their worth. Instead, piles of bodies of dead children became the terrible outcome of such results.

Operation Midnight Climax

The CIA, in the mid-sixties, wanted to study the concept and outcomes of LSD on students and civilians. The idea was that the agency wanted a leveraging study on drug trafficking, sex trafficking and the conduct of sexual abuses in the city of Los Angelo's and Washington. The agency would hire female prostitutes and they would send it would send the females to the rooms of drug lords. The prostitutes would contaminate the situations for the lords and gradually, compel them to spill the beans for drug trafficking. Here, dark psychology was passing with the concept of Dark Factor, where the agency, on the behest of its authority, wanted to have a command on the drug lords.

The Monster Study

This study was carried out by Dr. Wendell Johnson and Mary Tudor and they studied twenty-two children with imperfect care and zeal. They brought the children to their houses and created two group of children. One group was given positive speech notes and they were praised for their slight bit of contribution while speaking. The other group was a negative a speech note, where every word of the child, was belittled and defamed. The outcomes of this study were dark as well, because the children's mental cognition and behavioral practices never became as per the requirements of a sane individual and the research became very petrified about this. This Monster Study was never really published because of the fear that the researchers might get arrested of it.

Project MKUltra

From the year 1953 to 1973, the United States conducted a series of manipulating experiments for their citizens. The reason for such experiments were to induce, excessive drug use, the use of harsh words, emotional abuse, sexual abuse, psychological abuse and what not. The results became very hedonistic in their nature and ultimately the cases and subjects were meant to be shut down. The project MKUltra was halted by the Congress and in time, it was politically removed for the betterment of society.

The Aversion Project

This historical dark process was a landmark in Dark continuum. The apartheid era in South Africa was on its horizon and many people had to be displaced from their homelands seeking refugee in neighboring countries. The spree of homosexuality was prevalent in South Africa and they wanted to cure themselves in a therapist manner. Dr. Aubrey Levin was put in charge by the government of USA to cure the plight of the homosexuals. According to the doctor back then, the people of homosexuals were facing a mental disorder due to which, the homosexuals were unable to cure themselves. They started fleeing themselves away and doctor wanted to erase their sexual orientation by making them realize the harms of being a homosexual. The idea was that the homos must be displaced with nude pictures of gays and lesbians and they will be forced to curse them. Doing this, will make them unable to have any kind of love affiliation with any gay and they will feel all great and strong. Therefore, the aversion project was done on the sole purpose that how gays and lesbians are evil and bad in their utter character and quite possibly, this project can lead to success and sustenance.

Unnecessary Sexual Reassignment

Sexual Reassignment is a process, which tends to reassign and alter the sex of an individual through biological and scientific means. This process came to limelight when a nine-year-old boy's gender was reassigned as doctors were not sure of his apparent gender. His penis was circumcised during a mental process and with the passage of time, he had to be reassigned further. This trauma was a sever condition for the parents and they did not know what measures they need to adopt to finish this problem. They want to the doctors bashing their claims and the people had to face some observations regarding this matter as well. Therefore, this was a dark process, which was made to induce a horror spirit in the children of people so that they could remain an isolation in their approach.

Stanford Prison Experiment

This experiment was conducted in the midst of 1971, where prisoners and guard men were able to speak to one another and the people had to face the moral outcome of it. The idea was there needing to be the causes depiction between prisoners and guards and then their culture of interaction could be studied better. The people, who had been given the role of guard were taking their respective genres in a bad manner. The prisoners began to enforce harsh measures on the guards and the guards were not able to confess the suitability of that as well. The prisoners accepted the abuses in a rational manner and the people had to flee away from the cause by all means necessary.

Milgram Experiment

This experiment was conducted to understand the nature of Nazis, after the world war two. This Milgram experiment was designed to see if the patient is able to see the harsh realities of life and can be conform to the authority or not. There was a test tube that was placed on the sides of the patient and a questioning panel was placed in front of him. The panel asked some nefarious questions to him and made him realize that he was quite incompetent and could not able to answer good and subtle answers. This proved a dark mechanism in the minds of the people and the panel that psychology is very relevant in the scenario of people. Therefore, the Milgram experiment was a torturing way to express sorrow and sadness in the minds of people and hence, it was expunged off or halted by the people by all means necessary.

The Monkey Drug Trials

This event was an epitome of dark psychology in which animals were tested. They were injected with drugs and the outcomes of drugs were carefully examined by the public. The public rendered its advices to the people and made sure that how the reaction would lead the animals. This reaction was a necessary ingredient of the testing of animals and it was asserted in the means of people by all means necessary. The monkey trial gave a dark side of psychology to the public and with the passage of time, it was assured that monkeys are detriment to the society. Therefore, the monkey drug trials exhibited a darker version of the animals as well and people came to this result very quickly.

Facial Expressions Experiment

This experiment was conducted on the basis of studying the facial expression of people while providing them an external stimulus. In this experiment, it was asserted that people that have some mental troubling issues will be given an external stimulus so that the persons are able to have an impact of it. The facial expressions are there to judge the internal conditions of the individuals and then the personalities of the individuals are carefully assessed. The system is quite inherent in this manner and the people are able to give proper justification to the external responses. The external responses include the use of drugs, porn movies, the inducing of drugs and devastation and many more. The facial expression experiment gives the students and the clients a justification that the people are not able to have a sustainable present in them.

Little Albert

This was the dark hour of the psychological era. The founder of behaviorism, Mr. John Watson was deemed as the dark executor of this regime and he named some of the children to be equally liable in this regard. He would take a young child in his custody and he would test the abilities of him. Little baby albert was exposed to many sounds and other stimulus, which made him feel quite bad and slurry. This was done to condition fear of little albert and with the passage of time,

Albert was made quite inhumane in this regard. Therefore, little albert had to be taught something great about the channeling of darkness and atrocity in the present and with the passage of time, dark psychology made this landmark achievement that psychology can also be used to condition fear and badness.

Bobo Doll Experiment

This experiment was conducted to see the violent learnt behavior of children. Seventy-five children were taken from the primary school and they were positioned in the market to get more and more insight about the dark nature of the children. Dr. Albert Bandura was the psychologist in the experiment and he was given a strong assurance of the child's psyche and the child needs to be given more and more creativity to the matter of the children. Bandura repeated the experiment twice in the reflection of the students and it seemed like the children did not like it as well.

The results were that the children were continuously affected by dark continuum and dark myths and they were made to resolve to the experiments in an effective manner.

Conclusion

To conclude the book, dark psychology is the science that is used to induce horror and terror in the society. There are certain dark entities in the picture of the dark psychology, there are modes of dark psychology and then there is a strong version of dark history in the past, which shakes the crux of all individuals. The manipulation is an ardent job of the dark psychology and there are may ways for a manipulator to be used effectively. The techniques of dark control, dark seduction and dark mind control are haunting as well. There are characteristics of manipulators that can be very detrimental for its use and thus, the use of manipulation can be drawn in a major way forward. There are brainwashing techniques that set to imbue a structure of horror in the individual and then there is a demeaning process of dark triad, which could be equally horrendous. Therefore, in order to avoid the concept of dark psychology, it is pertinent to understand that the manipulators are all prevalent in the market and the society and one has to avoid them using, good deeds and efforts.

MIND CONTROL

Deepening of a Dark Psychology Technique:

How to Control People, NLP, Persuasion,

Mental Defense Systems, Mental Tricks,

Brainwashing, Manipulation, Dark Seduction

FRIEDRICH LLOYD

Table of Contents

Chapter 1 Introduction

This book is all about Mind Control. Mind control is a tool and a phenomenon, in which the cognition of any individual is controlled through external means. There could be internal and external factors that could lead to mind control and there are various nefarious tools that have been employed in this context. There is the use of Mind Control and vibrant manipulation that make the individual prone to hallucination and victimization. These processes have been bolstered by scientific experiments as well, where the subject was deciphered to understand the ins and outs of its minds. Also, there have been medieval experiments that showcase the use of Mind control for their own purposes and this book shall briefly argue about the use and crux of Mind control.

A brief contribution to the definition of Mind control will be given. Various assertions, by prolific authors will be discussed by many researchers and their contributions will be holistically discussed. Various historical events that harshly depict mind controls will also be elaborated along with some emphasis on dark psychology as well. The use of mind control will also be constructed in order to delve into this preposition that how Mind control tries to manipulate the emotions of the persons and what kind of personalities use for their demonic purpose. Furthermore, the use of emotional anxiety, the manipulation of heart routes and the use of bad omes will be discussed that how do they fall in the ambit of compassion. Therefore, the use of mind control will be revered in the chapters of the book with full brevity.

Moreover, the uses and types of mind control will also be discussed. Types of mind control mean that how the use of dark mindsets and other controlling aspirations will be utilized with full zeal and courage. The mind of the dark is the eccentric philosophy of the concrete people due to which the labor is able to be masqueraded in this regard. The mind control technologies can be constructed in a proper dimension and with the passage of time, the use is being further construed. Thus, a minor portion of this book will also look into the constructs of type of mind control as well.

Mind control technologies mean that how the person is able to have its best share of maneuvering with the people and the passage of time can also be inducted in many ways as well. The mind control technologies include the concepts of generalizations, gaslighting and smear campaigns that can give more and more emphasis to the mind control lobby. The use of triangulation and aggression can be useful for further personalities and with the passage of time, it could be used to deter the persona of other people as well. Mind control technologies will give you more credence and adherence to the regard and hence, it will be very suggestive in the coming. The use of mind control technologies could be detrimental in its nature and it will lead the minds of the people in a bad way possible.

Dangers of Mind control

The dangers of Mind control are as follows:

1. Mind control is secretive manipulation

The psychologists often compare mind control with brainwashing and they call both of them as different. According to the psychologists, mind control is the secret manipulation of someone to chaos and disruption. Apparently, the person is not able to see the difference properly but with the passage of time, Mind control tends to exist and the manipulator succeeds in having its contracts properly. Also, mind control tends to happen in any condition as well. At times, individuals are being innocuous as well and they do not know how to harbor the acceptability possibly, therefore; mind control will be able to give more assertions to the person systematically.

2. It is a gun to the head

Mind control is often interpreted as a compulsive gun to ahead. A person, who is under the conviction of someone else, is not able to have a proper version of it and with the passage of time, there is a strong gun to the head, which ultimately befalls the person from his end and attire. This is a controlling gun to the head of the persons, which makes him feel very bad and obscene.

3. Susceptibility

Susceptibility means that the person, who is using Mind control is trying to gain your control. He wants to accomplish his internal motives and wants to imbue horror in your character. He believes that you are the actual pawn of his style and he would do anything with you to get all the qualities of his motive. For susceptibility, it is important to figure out the mind constraints of people and with the passage of time, the manipulator is easy to get it done by all. Therefore, susceptibility is all the true nature of a human god and by important means, the person is able to get it.

Chapter 2 What is Mind Control?

Mind Control is an evil thing. It is the demonic attribute through which persons manipulate and marginalize another person's identity and cultural values. The arts and tactics through which the person is manipulated contain the use of obscene language, pre-planned unethical gestures, evil diplomatic maneuvers, malicious propaganda and many more. These tactics work on contrary basis to creativity. According to Blattino (1999), Mind Control is a mode of applying worst creative means in order to enslave the conscience of a normal personality. This means that if the person is under a trap of dark minds and negative people, then the bad people will use bad omens and gestures in order to embed the mind of the pure person in treachery and theft. This can be done through false propagation of information and other information outlets.

For instance, the person has not committed murder and his nemesis plot something vindictive for him through propaganda and he falls in it then this gesture will be considered a dark psychological motive for the person, who is in shambles now.

Signs of Mind control

Following are the five signs used for Mind control

1. Isolation

If you find yourself truly been isolated from the clout then it is the sign of mind control and manipulation. This means that someone is trying to use mind control against you and you are about to be put in shambles and systematic chaos. The isolation techniques are very haunting in their design and there will be use of extensive parameters to boost isolation and grumbling in the friend zone of yours. A common example can be use of bad tactics and backbiting of you so that no one in the group may have strong comfortability with you. This is the use of isolation and it is a renowned technique of Mind control.

2. Moody Behavior

The use of Moody Behavior can be used as a strong tactic to give isolation to the group. For instance, the mind-controlling man is becoming all moody and hawkish in his gestures. He will give you a notice of it and will remind you that you have not been able to make strong connections with him. In this way, you are inducing a sense of isolation and fragmentation in him and thus, he is becoming all moody in his character. This sort of moodiness means that you are not able to have a strong behavior of connection with him and he is already to manipulate you badly. Therefore, Moody Behaviour is all bad and bodacious in its way and hence, the public is able to be manipulated by it. Thus, the moody behavior needs to be vested in all possible means holistically.

3. Metacommunication

It is the sign of metacommunication in which the person is not able to induce proper communication with important gestures. For instance, the husband and his wife had a domestic with other personalities and a person was not able to give strong improvisations in the coming. The use of metacommunication can give a strong gesture of manipulation to the public and the people are able to have a lethargic sense of going through it. The use of Metacommunication can often occur in bad ways, where the person is not able to give proper signatures and abilities in a compatible manner. Therefore, the use of metacommunication is a strong tactic and tool used to manipulate people.

4. The use of Neuro-linguistic programming

The use of neuro-linguistic programming is a tool that can be used to induce thoughts into the language of the person and the person then uses the programming constructs to deliver better impacts to the people. The use of neuro-linguistic programming is another feature of programming that comes under the ambit of programming as well. The programming is used in many contexts and purposes and the programmer is able to have a sound knowledge of the other person as well. In this set of programming, the person is able to not understand the real reasons for manipulation and hence, the people come in a dark psyche of manipulation. Therefore, the use of neuro-linguistic programming helps you to govern the prospects of mind control and if you really are a mind controller, then this prospect is best for you.

5. Uncompromising Rules

If someone is making you comprise their rules and your rules as well then he is uncompromising. The uncompromising means that the person is able to make huge assertions in the mistake and with the passage of time, the person wants to instill hardcore breaks in it. The hardcore breaks tend to induce more issues in the people and hence, there is staunch manipulation in the minds of the public. Therefore, the uncompromising of rules is a way to manipulate people in an effective manner.

Chapter 3 A brief historical excursus on mind control

Freud's interest in Young Woman

This was the experiment that was conducted on the behest of Freud's relations with young women. In his Dark continuum, Freud believed that women, who do excessive masturbation are designed to be bad in nature and this is an ill-coordinated exercise that needs to be stopped. His experiments were many young women and out of them, was a young lady named, Emma. Emma had problems with anxiety and depression and she used to do a lot of masturbation just to make the pain go away and ace the mental trauma. She decided that she will never ever dare to pursue a relationship and in order to ace herself, she went for a doctor, who happened to be Freud. Freud made her inhale serious nostril drugs, which made her go dizzy and how was she treated, remained a mystery for long. The concept of Mind of the dark can be seen in these experiments, where Freud is testing the enduring skills of Emma and wants to carry on the experiment at the cost of every result. The mind control process is clearly exhibited in this experiment and such kind of tendencies are easily put forward in the mind of other people.

Electroshock Therapy on Children

Dr. Lauretta Bender of the Creedmoor Hospital believed that children, who do not have any social order in their characters are prone to be tested under an electroshock machine. She would invite many students to her lab and would not see the problems of the children clearly rather would ask some tough questions that would draw children towards the confusion. When the children aren't able to answer it then she would put them under an electroshock computer and with the passage of time, the children would lose their subconsciousness and be paranoid. This aspect, according to Dr. Lauretta was a tool to make the children active and strong but, in its progression, the experiments proved their worth. Instead, piles of bodies of dead children became the terrible outcome of such results. This is the kind of therapy, where the person is able to have a strong version of its concepts practically and it can be put under the ambit of mind control effectively. The use of mind control can take the persons to strong limelight and with the passage of time, there are many assertions and comprehensions in it.

Operation Midnight Climax

The CIA, in the mid-sixties, wanted to study the concept and outcomes of LSD on students and civilians. The idea was that the agency wanted a leveraging study on drug trafficking, sex trafficking and the conduct of sexual abuses in the city of Los Angeles and Washington. The agency would hire female prostitutes and they would send it would send the females to the rooms of drug lords. The prostitutes would contaminate the situations for the lords and gradually, compel them to spill the beans for drug trafficking. Here, Mind Control was passing with the concept of Controlling the Factor of Mind , where the agency, on the behest of its authority, wanted to have a command on the drug lords. Mind control of mind and personality is clearly put forward in this experiment, where people are able to have a strong version of personality frameworking of it. The use of operation can lead to a strong process of cultivation in it and hence, with the passage of time, the midnight climax would lead to proper assertions in the person.

The Monster Study

This study was carried out by Dr. Wendell Johnson and Mary Tudor and they studied twenty-two children with imperfect care and zeal. They brought the children to their houses and created two groups of children. One group was given positive speech notes and they were praised for their slight bit of contribution while speaking. The other group was a negative speech note, where every word of the child, was belittled and defamed. The outcomes of this study were dark as well, because the children's mental cognition and behavioral practices never became as per the requirements of a sane individual and the research became very petrified about this. This Monster Study was never really published because of the fear that the researchers might get arrested for it. The mind control was the main pillar of this study and the people wanted to make good assertions in this regard to the public. This was done to make the process look all good and pale. Therefore, mind control is implemented in this experiment effectively.

Project MKUltra

From the year 1953 to 1973, the United States conducted a series of manipulating experiments for their citizens. The reason for such experiments was to induce, excessive drug use, the use of harsh words, emotional abuse, sexual abuse, psychological abuse and whatnot. The results became very hedonistic in their nature and ultimately the cases and subjects were meant to be shut down. The project MKUltra was halted by Congress and in time, it was politically removed for the betterment of society.

The Aversion Project

This historical dark process was a landmark in Dark continuum. The apartheid era in South Africa was on its horizon and many people had to be displaced from their homelands seeking refugee in neighboring countries. The spree of homosexuality was prevalent in South Africa and they wanted to cure themselves in a therapist manner. Dr. Aubrey Levin was put in charge by the government of the USA to cure the plight of homosexuals. According to the doctor back then, the people of homosexuals were facing a mental disorder due to which, homosexuals were unable to cure themselves. They started fleeing themselves away and doctor wanted to erase their sexual orientation by making them realize the harms of being a homosexual. The idea was that the homos must be displaced with nude pictures of gays and lesbians and they will be forced to curse them. Doing this, will make them unable to have any kind of love affiliation with any gay and they will feel all great and strong. Therefore, the aversion project was done on the sole purpose of how gays and lesbians are evil and bad in their utter character and quite possibly, this project can lead to success and sustenance. The use of Mind control is another demeanor of the humans and with the passage of time, there are many experimentations in the public through which the public is able to have a sound mode of mind control. The mind control is an experiment that can be used to make the humans and other frameworks look more great and assertion.

Unnecessary Sexual Reassignment

This process is a heinous work of mind control. In this experiment, the mind control of the public is directly controlled and the person is able to have a lasting impact on the persons effectively. The effect of such a gesture will create more tendencies in the mind of the public and with the passage of time, the person has to be very cordial in its structure. Sexual Reassignment is a process, which tends to reassign and alter the sex of an individual through biological and scientific means. This process came to limelight when a nine-year-old boy's gender was reassigned as doctors were not sure of his apparent gender. His penis was circumcised during a mental process and with the passage of time, he had to be reassigned further. This trauma was a severe condition for the parents and they did not know what measures they need to adopt to finish this problem. They want to the doctors bashing their claims and the people had to face some observations regarding this matter as well. Therefore, this was a dark process, which was made to induce a horror spirit in the children of people so that they could remain an isolation in their approach.

Stanford Prison Experiment

The idea is simple in its research. This experiment was conducted in the midst of 1971, where prisoners and guard men were able to speak to one another and the people had to face the moral outcome of it. It is important to understand that the mind-controlling phenomenon of the prisoners and it is used to make the public go efficient about the mind game of the people. The idea was there needing to be the depiction of the cause between prisoners and guards and then their culture of interaction could be studied better. The people, who had been given the role of guard were taking their respective genres in a bad manner. The prisoners began to enforce harsh measures on the guards and the guards were not able to confess the suitability of that as well. The prisoners accepted the abuses in a rational manner and the people had to flee away from the cause by all means necessary.

Milgram Experiment

Mind control was used to be done in order to make the conduct of the person more reliable and efficient in its making. This experiment was used to see the level of assessment of the public and with the process of time, it created more realms of study. This experiment was conducted to understand the nature of the

Nazis, after world war two. This Milgram experiment was designed to see if the patient is able to see the harsh realities of life and can be conform to the authority or not. There was a test tube that was placed on the sides of the patient and a questioning panel was placed in front of him. The panel asked some nefarious questions to him and made him realize that he was quite incompetent and could not able to answer good and subtle answers. This proved a dark mechanism in the minds of the people and the panel that psychology is very relevant in the scenario of people. Therefore, the Milgram experiment was a torturing way to express sorrow and sadness in the minds of people and hence, it was expunged off or halted by the people by all means necessary.

The Monkey Drug Trials

This event was an epitome of Mind Control in which animals were tested. They were injected with drugs and the outcomes of drugs were carefully examined by the public.

The public rendered its advice to the people and made sure that how the reaction would lead the animals. This reaction was a necessary ingredient of the testing of animals and it was asserted in the means of people by all means necessary. The monkey trial gave a dark side of psychology to the public and with the passage of time, it was assured that monkeys are detriment to society. Therefore, the monkey drug trials exhibited a darker version of the animals as well and people came to this result very quickly.

Facial Expressions Experiment

This experiment was conducted on the basis of studying the facial expression of people while providing them an external stimulus. In this experiment, it was asserted that people that have some mental troubling issues will be given an external stimulus so that the persons are able to have an impact on it. The facial expressions are there to judge the internal conditions of the individuals and then the personalities of the individuals are carefully assessed. The system is quite inherent in this manner and the people are able to give proper justification to the external responses. The external responses include the use of drugs, porn movies, the inducing of drugs and devastation and many more. The facial expression experiment gives the students and the clients a justification that the people are not able to have a sustainable presence in them.

Little Albert

This was the dark hour of the psychological era. The founder of behaviorism, Mr. John Watson was deemed as the dark executor of this regime and he named some of the children to be equally liable in this regard. He would take a young child in his custody and he would test the abilities of him. Little baby Albert was exposed to many sounds and other stimulus, which made him feel quite bad and slurry. This was done to condition fear of little Albert and with the passage of time, Albert was made quite inhumane in this regard. Therefore, little Albert had to be taught something great about the channeling of darkness and atrocity in the present and with the passage of time, Mind Control made this landmark achievement that psychology can also be used to condition fear and badness.

Chapter 4 Where is Mind control used

Mind control is used in the following conditions:

The use of Homecourt

This is the manipulation technique in which the individual uses his or her home as an advantage for his own benefits. The psychological demeanor was used to define the crux of the people, who were under the liability of the people. For the substantiation of this case, it is important to understand that the people, who are in a psychological condition to manipulate others are very smart. The first rule is that the public must come into consideration of the psychological master and then the master will navigate his thoughts. First and foremost, the master uses the court to manipulate the personalities and then the public first advocate the use of manipulation to be just and obscure.

Establishing the stance first and then looking for weaknesses

In the manipulation of psychology, it is important to understand that the establishment of the stance is first. The stance needs to be manifested first and then it is established so that the people, who are listening to the track come under the way of the manipulator. Once the stance of the manipulator is established then the maneuvering is very easy. The people have to understand the use of the stance easily and then they have to use the words of the manipulator as a source of manipulation. The people can easily be thrown into abyss when the manipulator asks a lot of questions. The idea is that the public first navigates the stance and then the manipulator can use the stance to find its justification. If the manipulator wants to find the essence of the stance and if he finds some distortion of the stance then he can avoid the crux of the stance very badly.

Manipulation of Facts

If you want to assert the significance of the psychology of manipulation, then the facts stated can be used to deceive. The facts can be of any statement and that can be used to defy the logic of the people. For instance, if the manipulator is using the fact sound of one thing then that thing can be used to defy as well. Persons that can assess the logic of the personalities can manipulate by navigating them through their own lies. This is the act of manipulation if people are using the effects of deviance in an effective manner.

Overwhelming with facts and statistics

First and foremost, the fact and statistics can be used to defy the personalities of the public.

The facts are to be constructed in an effective manner so that the manipulator can be used to defy the odds of manipulation. So, for a strong manipulation, you have to overwhelm the facts and statistics with the persons. The persons can be used to come under the clout of statistics if the public is not able to use strong mode of psychological messages. Therefore, it is important that psychology can be used to interpret the essence of the public in a logical manner.

Overwhelming with procedures and Red tape

In order to maintain the crux of other personalities, the manipulator uses procedures and red tapes to give more defying reasons to the public. The manipulator will use the procedural versions, in which the public has to be manipulated in a stringent manner. The manipulator can be harnessed in a strong way so that the public can give concrete methods to it. For this reason, to be constructed, the manipulator uses some procedures and advantages through which the normal public comes into oppression. This oppression is used to defy the lands of the public and the public comes under the manipulation of the manipulator. So, in order to manipulate the people, the psychologists can use the crux of procedures and some secretive tapes that can be used in a strong manner.

Raising the voice and Displaying Negative Emotions

The manipulator in order to make the voice of the public effective has to raise the voice of himself. The manipulator uses some strong means and modes through which he is able to forecast a shadow of darkness. This darkness is used to construct the methods of manipulation among the stakeholders and the people can come under effective modes of destruction. Also, the negative emotions, give the value of harsh realities among the public and they get severely neglected by the personalities. Therefore, it is important to understand that the public is not able to get manipulated if they see the raised level of voice and hence there is a display of festering emotions among the people.

Negative Surprises

The negative surprises are another mode of manipulation by the manipulator. The manipulate can be using harsh negative surprises through which the people are not able to understand their nature. These negative surprises also affect the effects of mentality of the public and with the passage of time, the people do not get easily comfortable in this essence. The negative surprises show a strong moment of disinterest among the public and there is a culture of disassociation among the public through the negative surprises. The negative surprises give a sense of bad omens for the public through which the people are not able to give standard modes of deviation for the public.

Giving you a little or no time to decide

The time that has been given to you is either less time or there is no time. The manipulator wants to get his thing done because only then he is effective in his mode. The manipulator would cast his own means to come in front of the public. The time that has been slotted for the manipulator has a strong version of connectedness with the people and thus, there needs to be a strong sense of affection for the people. Therefore, the time of decision that has been given to you is a tool of the manipulator so that the public is able to give more directions for the public. So, the time has to be a motive interest for the public to understand in an effective manner.

Use of Negative Humor

The negative humor is a manipulating tool to disassociate you from your being. The manipulator would cast a negative humor on you and will do his best in making you feel bad about the situation. This manipulation is further designed by the manipulator to disempower you and with its continuous bolstering, the use of negative humor could be very harsh and brutal for you. Therefore, the use of negative humor could be used to induce isolationism and fanaticism in the public and could be very pernicious for you as well. If the use of negative humor could be bad for you then manipulation could be a stringent maneuver to showcase in-effectiveness among you.

Consistent Judgement

The consistent judgment could be a harsh tactic to induce fright among you. The manipulator could use the essence of judgement to make you feel discomfort able. How it can be done? This is as follows: Suppose, you are sitting in a room and the manipulator is sitting in front of you and you are able to hear the statements of the manipulator and with the passage of time, the public is not able to define the essence of the judgments properly. The public is quite effective in harboring the essence of the manipulator and if the manipulator is successful is dissing you with his judgments then finally you are under his claw. The consistent judgment will make you feel very demotivated and with the passage of time, you will be feeling delusional.

Silent Treatments

When the manipulator wants to harbor his mechanism then he uses the edifice of silence. This silence is very haunting. It is very managerial and with the passage of time, it induces a bad version of manipulation among you. You get affected by the silence of the manipulator and in time, this becomes very pestering among you. The silent treatment is also very haunting at an individualistic level because at times, the public are not able to see the results of it in a discomforting manner. Therefore, the silent treatments can be used to haunt the premises of the individual in a bad manner.

Pretend Ignorance

The manipulators can be used to see the edifice of ignorance in them. The people can be used to see the harmful effects of ignorance and the public can come into the direct affiliation of the manipulator. The manipulator could be seen pretending like he is ignoring the answers of the public but he is actually bolstering the acts of manipulation for the public. Therefore, it is important to understand that the public must cater to this regard seriously and if anyone is seen being ignorant then he/she is using manipulation. Thus, the idea is simple over here, if a person is able to see the harmful effects of ignorance in it then he can see what can actually lead in to it. Therefore, it is necessary to understand that pretension of ignorance is actually a mode to attain the prospects of ignorance.

Guilt-Baiting

There is a strong perception that the manipulators can easily use the edifice of guilt baiting in them. This is the idea that makes the manipulator plays the victim card. The manipulator aims himself to be the victim caretaker and with the passage of time, he starts to play the victim card with full zeal. The idea is that the more victimhood the person has to play, the more he gets into wrong and unnecessary means and progression. Also, with the victim card, the public has to see what are the harms and ills of the people, therefore, it is important to understand that the manipulator can be used in some essence of the presence of the public to disapprove any of its matter.

Victimhood

There are some of the imaginal victim hood believes in the minds of the manipulator that make him believe that he is the actual victim. He gets so strangled by the cost of doing bad things, that he focuses himself to be totally bad and pugnacious. All these believes make the manipulator believe that he has been severe victim of the public and with the passage of time, the victim has to be addressed with empathy and sympathy. The sympathy starts with this belief that the people are able to have a great amount of interest for the public and the people. Therefore, the culture of victimhood is a mode of making the person feel empowered by self-asserting himself to be a victim.

So, these are some of the manipulation techniques used in psychology to deceive the personalities in the future.

Chapter 5 Types of mind control

Following are the three common type of Mind Control

Other modes of Mind Control

There are many other modes of Mind Control that need to be described as well in order to get a close look in the dark methods of psychology.

4. Dark Mindset

The Dark Mindset is a set of imaginary lines and circles through which the public is able to get a dark side of almost everything. These circles are based on thoughts, feelings and perceptions that can lead to the task of sadistic ion by a dark body. Once you are in this circle of violence, you are not able to feel purposeful or have any sort of ambition and aim in you. The psychological maneuvering of Mind Control can lead to mental past of illusion and fragmentation that can be horrendous in their making.

5. Controlling the Factor of Mind

The Controlling the Factor of Mind is an apparent real of possibilities and potentials that are provident in all forms of humans. The Controlling the Factor of Mind will make you feel terrible at times when you are morally or socially dysfunctional. The Controlling the Factor of Mind can even welcome a spree of negativity upon you due to which you will feel ashamed and be in shambles. The Controlling the Factor of Mind can cause a lot of tensions and agitation for you as well. Therefore, the Controlling the Factor of Mind is a dark emblem, which is stored in us and could lead all of us to horror and terror.

6. Mind of the dark

The Mind of the dark is a concept which will be related and comprehended in terms of Astro-physics and astrology. The singularity is a small and dense particle of the dark hole, which is present in the center of the hole and it has a minimum space of energy in it. The Mind of the dark believes that persons, who are inflicted by it are bound to suffer from the horrors of isolation and estrangement. There are at par with every condition of life and there is a considerable amount of distance in between them and the space that is coming to them.

11.　　Gaslighting

This is the technique that is used to see if the person's words sound like his actions or not. The gaslighting is a method that can be used to question the belief of the personality and with the passage of time, the person has to understand the use of this tool to use the manipulation effectively. There is a set of questions among the public, used by the manipulator to dodge the essence of the questions and with the passage of time, the entire scenario of the public changes with time all because of the gas questions, asked by the manipulator.

12.　　Generalizations

The generalizations of a manipulator are a strong sense of demotivation for the public to withstand. The manipulator easily generalizes all the terms and tactics that are employed on a social, economic and political factor and with the passage of time, the generalizations come with time. The generalizations are important enough for a manipulator for the student to understand the essence of all compatible reasons for the public and with the passage of time, the manipulator is able to see the distance of the public go far away. Therefore, the distance of the public from the real cause actually defines the status of the manipulator and with the manipulator can control a lot of sense through it. Therefore, the use of a generalizing matter creates more and more aspect for the students and civilians. Thus, the use of generalization gives impetus to the manipulator and with the passage of time, it can be more asserted in the coming. So, generalization can lead to a lot of trouble and menace for the student.

13. Moving the goal post

The manipulators have every right to deny your goal and ambition. They call it the moving of goal post and this is how the public is able induce bad and obscene mechanism to it. The goal post is the ambition of every man to cater to the fundamentally obsessed question of the incident and with the passage of time, the manipulator tends to de-track you from the quest at the earliest. The track is therefore a sense of motivation for you and you do not get enough style of aspiration for the students and civilians. The idea is quite simple that the public are able to create more satisfaction for the public and with the passage of time, the manipulators induce havoc as well.

14.   Changing   the subject

The manipulator would do his best in changing the subject. This aspect makes avoid accountability of his previous actions and with the passage of time, he learns the act of treachery and deception. Any time or anyplace, where he is not able to see the masterpiece of the subject, he tends to foil with the public and therefore, he is not even governing to the matter of the public so that he could not even to the matter of appreciation. Thus, changing the subject of any conversation is also a tool of manipulation that is required by all means necessary.

15.   Name-calling

Name-calling is an art and tactic that can be used to induce marginalization in the incident and with the passage of time, it could lead to dilemmas and destruction. The name-calling starts with a mode of aspiration for the pupils but ends in utter destruction for the public. This concept can be easily seen in many areas and portions of the world and such a practice can induce horror and terror in the region. This practice of name-calling can be used in the factors that enable one with destruction and devastation.

16.   Smear Campaigns

This campaign is used to address the horrendous use of psychology for the public. This is a play in which you are the victim and they are the martyr. According to them, you have displayed a sense of bad relationship to them and for that mere reason they have labeled you as a dead person. You no longer have a sense of reputation in the system and every time you encounter them, they tend to call you bad and the gone one. This aspect has many difficulties for you and end up being a psychopath. This aspect has emotional issues for you, psychological issues for you, ovulational and many more. Therefore, smear campaigns are personally made to make you feel bad and obscene and with the passage of time, you feel very hectic.

17.   Devaluation

This devaluation is not the currency devaluation but it is the human devaluation of yourself, you tend to be very bad and obsolete in your character that you embarrass every one's exes. You will as it is your pertinent duty to make the lives and ages of others feel embarrassing and with the passage of time, you control over your anger just to inflict punishment among the others. For instance, there was a time when people were able to cooperate with one another and could not try to defame others. However, with the burgeoning social media, people tend to decide the relationship of others by making them feel very degenerate. This is the crucial aspect of psychology, which could be very tumultuous for you and with the passage of time, he felt very bad and worse. Therefore, devaluation is meant to be an outlet of Mind Control and it can be very harmful for anyone, who does it.

18. Aggressive Jokes

Aggressive Jokes are the modes to make others look small and in shambles. These jokes could be of anything like the jokes on individuality, the jokes on society and the jokes on caste. These jokes impose derogatory remarks on the individuals and with the passage of time, the individuals feel very bad about them. The idea is simply that the psychology believes that manipulators could be worst nightmares for innocent personalities. People can use the edifice of others to personally sabotage the concept of friendliness and equality among the persons and with the passage of time, the people tend to showcase a system of defamation among others. Thus, aggressive jokes can be bad and hazardous for others.

19.   Triangulation

This is the concept, in which the individuals tend to use the supposed threat of others to manipulate the innocents. Suppose there are three individuals in a room, two of them are having an argument about anything and the person sitting next to them is of a high castc. The manipulator would use the edifice of supposed threat of the third person to deter that of a second person and with the passage of time, the concept of triangulation would be bolstered.   Hence, the use of force and manipulation is done in order to make the third parties very bad and degenerate.

20.   Use of tools

In this paragraph, the tools that can be used for manipulation will be discussed. These are sensory devices, visual sensor, automatic assembly, industrial manipulator and photoelectric detector. These tools cast a shadow of degeneration among the personalities and with the passage of time, the people are able to have list of traumata embedded in them. Therefore, with the passage of time the tools can be used for a stringent version of collaboration.

Thus, these are some of the ways and tools of manipulation that can harbor bad deeds in the person.

Chapter 7 Use of neuro-linguistic programming to improve self-esteem, manage one's feelings and believe in oneself

Neuro-Linguistic Programming

The use of neuro-linguistic programming is a method, which is used to cater to depression and anxiety. On an international level, the use of NLP is done in order to make the programming look more easier and effective. Following are some of the principles of making the process look more effective and good.

Techniques involved for NLP

1. Internal Maps of the world

The psychologists tries his best in making the people aware of their potentials. The internal map technique is a way forward to make the people fully involved in their making. The internal mapping is the concept of all body parts of the humans and the people are made aware of the concepts of fruition and productivity in them. The internal maps is a concept in which the people belonging to every aspect of the world are made more familiar to one another. The internal maps refer to all the body parts of the world, the language structure and the governing mechanism of the body. All these parts are interrelated and they are made more sound and sustainable in this regard. Therefore, it is important for the people to make the people make aware of the concepts involved in them.

2. Modeling

Modeling is a process in which the subject is told to model the behaviors, customs and languages of other people effectively. In this experiment, two models are made together in the concept and the people have to properly understand the structure holistically. The modeling comes with the passage of time and every behavior is carefully constructed so that the people are able to have a better understanding of the subjects. Therefore, modeling is a tool to induce more skeptic behaviouralism and with the passage of time, the people are able to come close to the mechanism effectively. Thus, modeling is an exercise, which can give proper illustrations with the passage of time.

3. Milton Model

Milton is a hyper-communication model, in which the person is able to have a computerized communication with Milton and Milton is a renowned psychologist as well. The psychologist helps to make the things in a proper manner and this Milton model will make you look effectively. The use of milton model will bring communication and character building of the individual and with the passage of time, the individual is able to make things more pragmatic in the coming. Thus, the Milton model makes the thing look more great and substantial in their matter.

4. Rapport

The rapport method is a type of method, which makes the belief of the personality look in a better manner. Rapport is the person, who has to be taken in the making of the individual and this is the process, which can make the individual look more dignified and designated. The ideas for this concept is very simple as it can provide good qualities to the individual.

Chapter 8 Who can be a victim of mind control?

The people that are prone to the following conditions can be under the emblem of Mind control

8. Plain Old bullying

If your partner or any individual in the relationship is trying to bully you then you are being the manipulated. The result of the manipulation will come late but the present bullying is the result that will make you go restless and repugnant to conciliation. You will feel that your entire life is in devastation and with the passage of time, you will tend to be more and more exhaustive. Thus, the concept of plain old bullying will be a hallmark of affection for you and you will feel very agitated in its regard.

9. Home Court Advantage

In any manipulation, the victim can understand its victimhood if the person is playing his home-court advantage. This means that the person is not able to see the charms of life in a pleasant manner and he is feeling all bad and bodacious about it. The home-court advantage makes him go restless and in the passage of time, the manipulation gets stronger. Thus, the use of home court advantage is a reflection of manipulation.

10. If you really cared about me

This technique grants a skeptic though to the manipulator that in order to make him more and more compulsive, he starts to ask more questions like if you had really cared about me and made me feel very great. If you had made me not so uncomfortable in the past and like how you can necessarily give more weight in this regard. The idea to this method is one has to be very relaxed in the confession and keeps on avoiding any such statements, which can make him more and more instrumental in this regard.

11.   Emotionally Blackmail

The emotional blackmailing is an aspect, which will have a lot of confusions for you in the coming. It will make you feel more and more inspirational in the coming and hence, you will be able to have a sound connection of emotions with you. The emotional blackmailing, if it is present then it can make the wills look bad and in times, it can make thing go in an effective manner. Therefore, the emotionally blackmailing is an aspect of manipulation and if it is prevalent in your relationship then you are being manipulated to a large extent.

## 12.	Convenient Neediness

This neediness is the method, which is only done on convenience for the people. The manipulators will be using the convenient card to make the people be aware of the masses of the public and with the respect of time, it is mandatory for the people to get to the affection in a certain manner. The convenience helps the manipulators to help the message of their utility go in a start manner. Therefore, if you want to have a convenient bases of neediness in you then you can actually help others to achieve the best possible way possible.

## 13.	Killing them with kindness

The kindness helps the individuals to know about the surface of the individuals. The manipulators use the edifice of kindness in a perpetual manner. The people will tend to look into the matter of others by possibly making them a culprit of their kindness and thus, the individuals can look into the regard in a possible manner. The manipulators would kill their relationships in a continuous way and hence, the people will come to know the edifice of kindness in a fair manner. Therefore, killing them with kindness will make the pupil know more and more about the just policies effectively. Hence, the killing aspect makes the kind gestures more productive and potential.

14.   Very calm at the starting

The students tend to be very calm about the people all in the making. They make the individual more kind in their collection and the individuals make the aspect of kindness in a just manner. Therefore, the manipulators will be kind to you and if you want to make the best of the process. Try your best in making them manipulators go away.

Following tips can be used to control people.

14.   He is charming and nice

The manipulator is all charm and nice at first. He would try his best in making you feel comfortable and gradually, he would impart his shrewdness. First, he would come in your comfort zone by wishing you birthdays, by giving you gifts and making you feel less agitated about anything then he would cast his dogmas. Once he knows that you will not bother him about anything then he would tell you to do anything by all means necessary. Sometimes, his manipulation is so strong and stringent that he can make you do anything even a murder. Thus, this is the idea of manipulation that is started with charming voices and ending in catastrophe. Beware of such people.

15.   Denial

The manipulator would always deny any assertion or statement of guilty on him. He would be felt exempt of any charges and would dare to see himself in the crux of any problem. If you somehow even manage to bring him in any disaster then he would just simply run away and would assert his innocence overcharges. He would think of himself as a strong mode of eccentricity and he would deny any kind of charges on him and would plead his innocence all over time. This is the true nature of denial that it tends to be very compulsive and bad in its progression and becomes haunting as well. Therefore, the denial is able to make the people look very bad and obsolete to the individual.

16.   Lying

The people are able to lie a lot and those, who can actually conform themselves on it are lying. The lying edifice starts with the inculcation of hate speech and derogation and with the passage of time, the people tend to learn a lot of lying. The innocents are not able to see the manifestation of lying in their inner sides and they do not how exactly is the platform of lying quite degenerate about it. The lying helps the manipulator to learn more and more about the advances of the individual and with the passage of time, he comes one step closer tin dodging and abhorring you. This is the strong crux of lying that needs to be strengthened by all means necessary.

17.   Excessive Flattery

This sign is of huge importance with the manipulator. The manipulator is able to do a lot of flattery for the individuals and with the passage of time, the individual can harbor flattery and sweetness among the individuals. The flattery helps to manipulate the individuals in a strong manner and this flattery can be of any side and sustenance. The idea exhibited here is quite strong as the people are able to create an environment of justice and order in the citizens and the flattery helps to regulate themselves in an effective manner.

18.   Forced Teaming

The individual can use the teaming of the layers for his own motives. This teaming can be devious in its nature and can reflect many ills and whims of the societies. The teaming can also lead to a social segregation in the society and with the passage of time, the person can easily regulate its crux in a mature manner. The force teaming can appoint strong versions of impact for the students and with the passage of time, the individuals can come up with strong assertions. The forced teaming could be the use of any strength and value and it could be very destructive in its nature as well. Therefore, forced teaming is a sign of affection for the manipulator and it is destruction for the students as well.

19. Good First Impression

The manipulator will always do his best in making the best impression that he can in order to carefully influence the minds of other people. This is a well-managed task just to make sure that the audience is under the reflection of the manipulator and you will all means necessary, follow under the trap of the manipulators. The good impression can be very expressive in its command and it can yield to proper potential as well but its lasting impacts are very pernicious. With the subtle use of good impression, the person can easily establish his core links with you and can make you do almost everything. Therefore, a person having an expression of good impression in him will be interpreted as a manipulator.

20.   Pretending to be a victim

The manipulator is of a harsh and smart demeanor. He knows that if he will pretend to be a victim then all the persons will listen to him and no matter what are the conditions his stance and statements will stand correct. He will understand this assertion in a jiffy and will do his best in making the public very bad and obscene. The idea is simply that the person is not able to convey his true propositions to the public and he pretends to be a victim. The concept of victimhood tarnishes his image and with the passage of time, he tends to deviate from the straight path. This mere concept completely obstructs the use of empathy from the manipulator's mind and with the passage of time, he feels very degenerative. Therefore, the person, who is a manipulator, will always have sign of victimhood in him.

21.   Silent Treatment

This sign is of strong admiration in the person, who is playing to be a manipulator. The manipulator will easily treat the level of punishment to the audience and while doing this, he will be silent and stringent as hell. This is the idea of concealing and secrecy that the manipulator employees and with the passage of time, he is able to impart a devious mechanism of dealing thing upon the individual. Therefore, it is important to observe the silent treatment of things in the public and this silent treatment will actually make the person feel very atrocious. Therefore, in order to see the sign of manipulation the person has to be very silent and if he is found silent then yes, he is a manipulator.

22.   Appearing to be selfless

The signs of selflessness are the signs that make the individual look very harsh and strong. The selflessness comes in the individuals either he has a golden heart or is he using the emblem of selflessness for himself. For instance, a boy, who is a manipulator falls in love for a person and asserts her to be selfless. In the moment, perhaps he is vouching for a love affair but in true sense, he tends to be manipulative. He would cast the shadow of badness upon the girl just to have an advantage of her and even get something from her. Therefore, the use of selflessness is also a quality that needs to be strengthened properly.

23.   Guilt Tripping

The idea of guilt-tripping is essential to understand as to decipher the nature of manipulation. In the guilt-tripping, the manipulator harbors the power of guilt in an individual and with the passage of time, he manipulates the other individual uses his guilt. He showcases that he is no the one, who is guilty and he trips the momentary aspects of guilt just to convey his innocence. This is a culture of guilt-tripping and it is easily found in all the corners of the world. Even international leaders use the edifice of guilt-tripping to transcend a culture of guilt-tripping. Therefore, it is important to understand that guilt-tripping can lead to a devastating blow of injuries and badness.

24.   Shaming

When the manipulator easily acquires his motives, he starts shaming others. He feels that individual is of no worth and in order to destroy him completely, he must be shamed. He would shame you using harsh means, he would kill you possibly, he would employ derogatory remarks upon you and he would instill a culture of deviance among you.

Therefore, the culture of shaming is found prevalent among the manipulators and if one has to recognize a manipulator, then he can use this edifice for good reasons. This is the revering identity of the individuals by all means necessary.

25.   Intimidation

The person is able to intimidate the other personality if he is manipulative. The manipulation is a hectic task as it requires a lot of effort for the manipulator to intimidate you. This intimidation can be strong as it could lead to an effective mode of manipulation for the individuals. The intimidation starts with a turning point as it will create more efflux of opportunities for the personalities for you. This culture of intimidation is great as you can create more manipulative tactics for your self but in the end, it will be harsh for you. Therefore, it is mandatory to understand that intimidation is a recognizing aspect of a manipulator.

26.   Diversion

Diversion refers to the diversity of opinion among the manipulators so that the people can easily lead to a better productive scenario of people to people contact. This diversity is important for you as it will yield greater sense of affection for you and in the presence of time, you will be able to diversify your opinion based on a common strand of diversity. This means that the manipulator can use the edifice of diversity just to yield more manipulation and strength in him. This can be taken in the aspect of plurality of opinion and in many ways, it can be dangerous as well.

8. Do all the thinking

The manipulators will do their best in doing the thinking for you. They will think for you and will tell you the best for you. However, the doing revolves around the crux of manipulation. They are doing this so that you can be in their domain and thus, there mind control tactic is successful. This is the better prospect for you and once you do this, you are in the action of the mind control.

9. Starting an avalanche

The avalanche is a marketing firm that makes you strong and subtle in their regard. The creation of an avalanche is pertinent for you to understand and with the passage of time, there is a secret maneuvering for you and you will induce an avalanche for you. The avalanche for you is that you have to be in the claws of an avalanche for you. Therefore, the mindset of the individual is easily dodging and with the passage of time, he is able to have a control of the manipulator.

10.   Ask for an inch take a mile

The asking for an inch and taking a mile is a concept that asserts the importance of taking things quickly. This means that the manipulator would cast a shadow quickly and with the passage of time, he would ask things for you which would have no actual reasons. This can be explained with an example. The manipulator would do a big favor for you and in return, you would love to comply him and with the passage of time, the manipulator would not take your compliments. He would ask of something great and then he would take a profuse amount. This is the basic tenant of manipulation that ask something else and get all-in return.

## 11.	Always have real deadline

The real deadline means that the person has to realistically forecast a shadow line on you and you are not expected to do anything in return. The deadline means that you will do something for him and in return, he will give you proper isolation for you. Therefore, it is important to understand the nature of you and you will have the prospects in no time. The real deadline refers to the last concept of the material and with the passage of time, you will get a new result in the formation.

## 12.	Giving ten times more

The manipulator will be able to leverage himself by giving you more and more things. If he does something for you and in return you do better for him. Then this is the mode of affection for him. Therefore, the giving of ten-time will provide you a sustainable moment of affection for yourself. This is exactly the method of utilization for you and you will be able to have more relaxation of it. Therefore, the giving of more things is actually a way to control the minds of the public and he will get more and more insight of it. Thus, the giving of more and more things will provide you with better affection.

13.   Standing for something greater for you

The people are able to get in your mind control if they believe in you. In order for them to believe in you, you have to do something great for them. To an extent, that they will always recall of you while they are pursuing something and they are able to have a problem in any situation. In this way, they will harbor all the mechanisms for you that will induce a great sense of affection for you.

Therefore, the standing for something is actually an act of affection for you and the people around.

## 14.	Be shameless

The people are always shameless, who want to manipulate you carefully. They feel as it is their importance to have you onboard for their progression. They believe that the people will understand you effectively if they are shameless. Being shameless does not mean that they dance in all nudity for you but in actual terms, they are able to have a strong sense of affection for you. Therefore, being shameless is an attribute to you so that you are able to have a precautionary sense of affection in you.

## 15.	Eye seduction

In psychology, you can use the edifice of eye to eye connection in order to make the eyes look greater and more effective. The eye effect is important to seduce the other end of personalities. The personalities are able to have a great sense of seduction in them due to which the public is able to have fun and persuasion. The eye seduction is tantamount to give more and more value to the psychologists and in time, they are able to have more fun and zeal in the eye seduction. Thus, it is important to do eye seduction in the coming time.

# 16.	Using the lack nesses

In dark psychology, you can use the lack nesses of other personalities so that you can have the leverage on other personalities. You will understand in time that the individuals will be able to have more and more zeal in them. The lack nesses can give you more aspect in their clout. The clout can be more incisive in their regard. The use of edifice can help you give more and more aspiration in the coming. The psychologist and the manipulator will use this prospect to gain leverage in the coming time.

Chapter 11 How to convince people to do whatever you want

10.　Avoid contact with the manipulator

First and foremost, do your best in avoiding contact with the manipulator. This means that the manipulator has to be firm and fervent in this regard and you have to do your best in befriending them. You can also make the contact look very dismissal and there is no need for you to be socially devoid of them.

11.　Say no to being manipulated

You must not come in trust with manipulation. If there is a friend of you that is trying his best to manipulate him and then you must say no and must try your best in making the assertions look very bad. So that the individuals are able to make the stand at a far distance and you are not able make an assertion.

12. Ignore the words would be

Often the manipulator uses the words would be. You need to avoid and must never the listener build the case on it. The idea is simple that do not build any such statements and assertions that could be harmful for you. Therefore, you must do your best in ignoring the words would be and never let any issue try to harm or dismantle you. Therefore, the ignorance is important for you to understand so that you can yield a good life.

13. Always set personal boundaries

Never allow the manipulator to be at your personal side. Always set some personal boundaries, which will make you look very bad and obscene. Try your best in setting the personal boundaries of the people and make yourself look smart and stringent. Thus, the idea of setting personal boundaries will make you feel very confident and compound.

14.   Set goals and tell others to be away with them

The idea of setting goals will make you understand that you have a vision and an aim in life. The setting of goals will make the manipulator go away and he will not bother you no matter what. The idea starts with a potent moment of consideration and with the passage of time, it is important for you to refrain from any indulgence and incarceration. The setting of goals will help the manipulator to go away and the person will be able to have a lot of fun for himself.

15. Stay calm

Whenever you talk with a manipulator, you will notice that they will try to overcome your passion with respect to time. You have to stay calm and will be if you are able to create more strong versions of time. The idea of staying calm will make you fall apart from the manipulator and you will be at the epitome of your life with concentration.

16. Say no firmly

If there is a job from the manipulator and he tends to disarray you then you have to say no. No can be in words and in actions as well and can personally, make you feel very great. You will be able to leverage the personality maker and with the passage of time, you will see that the persons are able to have a sound knowledge of it as well. The manipulator, who is doing this thing will make you feel very robust and within times, you will get to know the aspects of it in a better way. So, say no to the individuals and with the passage of time, you will feel very great and effective.

17.   Assert   yourself and be hard

Assertion is a hard tactic for the manipulator to handle. The manipulation can be forsaken with anything and with the passage of time, the assertion can help you make more comfortable and relaxing in time. The assertion is a necessary thing as well and it can lead to a better personality as well. Therefore, the assertion needs to be commanded with full zeal and courage.

18.   Practice self-care

Always practice self-care, no matter what happens. You will understand that what is momentarily required to dodge a manipulator. The practice of self-care will make you feel very bad and with the respect of time, you will tend to be very strong and stringent. The idea is simply that you have to be very cohesive in your regard. The assertion is simply that one can lead to the prosperity of the question in a better way. The practice of self-care would be effective. Therefore, it is essential for you to understand the importance of self-care with full zeal and honor.

Chapter 12 How to open a door to a woman's heart

This chapter will look into a thesis that how the heart of a woman is won properly. Following are some of the reasons of that how the heart of a woman is won.

Ways to open a door to woman's heart

Following are the ways to open a door to a woman's heart

1. Always be Pursuant

If you want a girl and woman to be at your doorsteps then you have to be pursuant in all the matters possible. By being pursuant, it is important that you have to come close the woman's heart, you have to be close to the aspirations of the woman, must understand the needs and harbor the acts of women as well. You have to make sure that woman is able to have a strong persuasion in her desires and you need all the prospects of pursuing a woman, in a dignified manner. Therefore, being pursuant means that you have to understand the significance of the woman's existence and with the passage of time, you have to be independent with her by all means necessary.

2. Be a gentleman

Being a gentleman, there is important rule while being a gentleman. You have to understand the qualities of a queen in order to be a king and with the passage of time, you have to harbor strong means effectively. The prospects of gentlemen means that you must be able to give more and more credence to the value and must secure all the prospects in a complete manner. Thus, being a gentleman implies that you need to understand the qualities of noble man and listen to the women in a complete and compassionate manner.

3. Be complimentary

When it comes to handling, then you have to give all the respected compliments to her by all means necessary. You need to induce strong assertions in her that she believes in you and you two get along together. For instance, if she cooks something for you then you must comply with her about the taste of food and better ambiance. At any decision making, where she is giving her respective decisions, you must adore them and by all means necessary, you need to provide strong complementation to her by all means necessary.

4. Be creative

You need to be creative appreciating her and there should be not any issues whatsoever with her. You need to harbor creative appreciation as well for her. You need to induce a spirit of mobility for her and by all means, she will come close to your heart.

Creation further bolsters love connectivity with other people and therefore, love has the ability to induce more creation in the love sphere. Therefore, in order to make the creation more worthwhile it is important to understand the love affair with a woman and hence creatin comes with the passage of time.

5. Be intentional

The intention of a candidate is also judges in this regard and the husband has the discretion of the wife' love regime. The husband needs to be purely intentional in this regard and must have the ability to boost more love and adoration in the woman's heart. The ability to have the care for others is a sign of pure intent and hence, the intention of the man is carefully remembered in this regard as well.

6. Speak well of her in front of others

The husband needs to be well in front of others about his wife. In this way, the wife will be very motivated and the wife will be fall in strong love connection with the husband. The person will be able to have more connections with the person and with the passage of time, the husband and wife will have a strong mode of connection with other personalities effectively. However,if the person is not able to give proper concentration to the topic and is degrading the woman in front of others then there will be serious set back for her. Therefore, in order to be well put with the women, you need to be very active and zeal with the personalities.

7. Be very protective

You need to be very protective of your wife if you want to be more sustainable with her.

The only way for that is to value her with all the zeal and courage you have for her. You need to understand that how the love affair with your wife with vary with time and by doing this, you have to be totally comfortable in this regard and zeal. Therefore, it is important for you to make proper changes with your wife at any coming time and there needs to be no dilemmas and destructions with her by all means necessary. Thus, be very protective with her and have a strong love affair with purity and content.

8. Be a good listener

When you listen great you are able to have a strong relationship. Listening great makes you understand the inner voices of the woman, in a much-contended manner. These voices resonate in your heart and brain and with the passage of time, there is a strong connection with the lady by all means necessary. Good listening also creates a strong sense of coalition with the partner and with the passage of time, you are able to have a lasting effect with the wife. Therefore, be a good listener if you want to live a happy and creative life.

9. Be romantic

If you want to have a long-lasting romantic event with your wife then try to appreciate little things and feel pleasured about it. The little sayings of your wife when she is curling your hair, the strong rebukes when you do something bad and the bad repercussions for you if you tend to behave in a wrong manner. Therefore, it is important for you to boost romanticism in the culture of living with you wife and never be ashamed while romanticizing with your wife.

## 10.	Just be yourself

The most important thing to put in mind while having an affair is that you need to be yourself with your wife. Do not try to be overdramatic and tend to induce horror and terror with your wife. Do not act like you are not the person you think you are and always be more compatible with the wife of others if you think you can suffice. Therefore, it is important for you to be yourself and never let the assertions float in a negative manner. Thus, the use of individualistic aspect will make you look more acceptable and accurate.

So, these are the ways to open the door to a woman and you have to be very careful while you do this.

Chapter 13 Mental defense systems

There are some of the ways through which your mental system can act like a defense system to many allergic comments. You can use these ways to induce a halt to the mind control factors. These are as follows:

1. Repression

Repression means that you are about to forget the evil thoughts and mechanisms that could trigger agitation in you. You have to induce the spirit of repression in you so that you may able to forget all the bad thoughts and ideas that one has induced in you. You have to use the concept of acceptance and individualistic effort on you and therefore, you are able to have a stringent version of acceptance in you. Thus, repression acts as a strong defense mechanism and you are able to give viable justifications to it.

2. Projection

In this kind of a mental defense system, you have to project the positive feelings of any problem in front of you. You have to make sure that any negativity that comes into your mind is easily removed and you are able to have a solid grip on your comfortability of the thoughts. You need to make sure that any such ingredients that tend to distort your inner feelings are not hampered and are not projected in your mind. Therefore, the very idea of projecting good feelings in the situations of bad feelings is named as projection. Thus, you need to govern these instruments effectively in the manner.

3. Displacement

Displacement means that you need to empower the inner thoughts of yourself in an effective manner and by any yardstick, you need to be pragmatic in the developments. The displacement helps you to engage others in a positive manner and you are able to have a sound impressions of yourself. However, if you are not able to make a strong displacement of yourself then you are in the impression of the bad ones. Therefore, displacement helps you make the assertions come in an effective manner.

4. Rationalization

The rationalization mechanism works with the implementation of this principle that you need to come up with strong emotions in your brain. You can avoid any negativity in the atmosphere and most importantly, you cannot sustain without them either. You have to bolster rationalization in yourself so that you are able to have a sustainable feature of intellect in you. You need certain primaries in yourself while you are rationalizing. You have to be bold and independent in your saying and never let lose in front of others no matter what happens. Therefore, rationalization is a strong defense system that makes you believe in your self and no matter where you go, you are able to have a strong system of catering emotions through it.

5. Reaction Formation

The reaction formation is a concept, which indicates that once the negativity has been uttered upon you, you are able to form a reaction on it. The reaction is that you do not need to have a strong reservation about it but you must have the credibility of conjunction in you. The easiest way for you to form a reaction formation is that you need to believe in the formation of strong reactions. You can do them anytime in the coming time and you do not have to feel submerged while doing so. Therefore, the formation of reaction creation is another way to make way for strong opponents coming in the time.

6. Denial

In order to make the emotional mechanism of yourself up to date, you need to deny any such restrictions upon you and must do your best in denying any sort of imposition upon your character. For instance, if someone is imposing any alleged mark on you then you have to make the substance of the world in a reactive manner and must not bring the concepts of the loser in a bad way. Thus, the denying process is the process that cultivates emotional uprising in you and in order to make, the world a better place, you need to deny any such impositions on you.

7. Regression

This process means the minimum cultivation of negative process in you. You are able to dilute any such assertions in you that could lead to a catastrophe. You have to make or break the concept of affair in it and by the passage of time, you have to be very opportunistic in your desire. Thus, the process of regression is an important tools for you to make the negativity process go all away and you would be able to refurbish yourself in a primary matter.

8. Intellectualization

Intellectualization means that you need to provide an intellectual answer to all those chaos that could disrupt you badly. The intellectualization can come with strong potential making and can raise a bar for you for sure but you have to make it smart and interactive for yourself. The idea is simple and straight that in case of any negative emotions hampering you, you have to adjust your self effectively for the matter. Therefore, intellectualization comes with the evolutionary process and can be very binary for you in the coming time.

So, these are some of the defense mechanisms that could boost interaction for you in the coming and with the process of time, you can induce entertainment in the character of yourself if you are able to make things go prudently.

Chapter 14 How important is breathing control, voice control and thinking

Breathing control over your body is very important and mandatory in order to avoid any mind control issues. You need to be breathing in an effective manner, in order to salivate yourself. Following are some of the way to make the breathing all great and sound.

1. Breathing Diaphragrametically

When you are breathing diaphragmatically then you are able to control the gestures of Mind controlling agent. An agent no matter how bad and anxious he is, he will not be able to create a space of agitation for you. The breathing diaphragmatically order will always help you to create a job function for the coming and people and with the coming time, you will be able to unlock all the potentials of a good agent. Therefore, breathing diaphragmatically will make you feel sound and substantial in the coming.

2. Breathing boosts confidence

Breathing makes you align with the coming matters. The ability to have a proper set of confidence can have many experiences for you. When you are able to breathe properly then with the passage of time, the breathing will systematically inculcate confidence in you. The idea is that you are not able to have a stable confidence in you with the passage of time and thus, there will be underlying presence for you. Therefore, breathing confidence will make you do wonders and with the passage of time, you will feel very apparent.

3. Thinking makes you be yourself

The more you think and do things, the more you are able to form good connections. The more you are able to make think pragmatically, the more you are able to make things in an effective manner. Thinking makes you believe that everything is all right and you are able to have a great sense of affiliation. Thinking helps you delve into the process of thinking in a compatible manner and with the passage of time, thinking makes you upbring better compositions in a coming manner. Thus, thinking helps you be yourself and you are not devoid of mind control in the coming.

So, the importance of proper breathing and efficient thinking makes you believe that mind control will not come to you in a coming manner.

Chapter 15 Mental pharmacological control

The use of pharmacological control is the use of pharmacological medicines to curb the menace of mind control. The use of medicines that can be effectively curbed through mind control come in the ambit of Mental Pharmacological control.

Medicine involved

Following medicines are involved in the process of mind control.

1. Chlorpromazine

The use of chlorpromazine is very effective in the process of Mind control. Injection, Oral liquid and Tablet will help you to control mind control progressively. The dose is up to 25g, 25 mg and 100 mg in the collection and the implementation of proper drug control through it. The use of chlorpromazine will help you control the use of drug productively.

2. Fluphenazine

Fluphenazine is the medical drug, which will make you go with high standards effectively. The use of Fluephenzine will make you have a proper control of Mind control and dosage and with the passage of time, the drug will easily cater to this regard.

The way of prescribing

The way of prescribing is very easy when it comes to the remedification of mind control. The mind control is a process in which the people are able to have a medical dosage of drugs, which alleviates their processing and therefore, the prescription makes them much easier to be effectively happen. The prescription is also very cost-effective in its formation and therefore, the medical prescription will make the system more adaptable and coherent in its use. Thus, the mental pharmacological method is a way to have a proper dosage of instructions effectively.

7. Isolation

Isolation starts with the basics of brainwashing. The brainwashing is important to understand by the manipulator. The manipulator would use the edifice of isolation. The isolation is effective in its use and by all means necessary, the manipulator tends to isolate you from social order. He makes you understand that the world is not effective in its use and can be very haunting in its meaning. Therefore, isolation is a technique used to be understood effectively.

8. Attacks on self-esteem

While brainwashing, the manipulator uses the edifice of attacks on self-esteem. For him, the brain of you is of high importance. Whatever he thinks of you can be altered only if he wishes to change your brain. You will make the self-esteem of yourself and by the prospects you will understand that the manipulator is using this edifice to brainwash you.

9. Mental abuse

In order for the brainwashing to work more effectively, the use of mental abuse is of high importance. The use of mental abuse will work in a practical manner and will thwart the conformity of the brain precisely. The mental abuse can be used of mentality and effectively and with the passage of time, you will understand that you are seeking to feel very obscene. Therefore, the crux of mental abuse will be effective for you in its making.

10.   Physical abuse

The physical abuse will look into the brainwashing in a complete manner. Do your best in avoiding the physical abuse of the manipulators. Otherwise, you will find yourself in a turbulent manner. The physical abuse can lead to the tarnishing of the brain and you will feel very bad at the end. Therefore, the concept of physical abuse must never be allowed to be furnished at the first place.

11. Only allowing contact with selected members

Brainwashers or manipulators want you to contact with selected members. The selected members will cater to the brainwashing effectively and with the passage of time, they can be successful if you do not object them at the first place. The selected members will showcase a culture of degeneration among you and with the passage of time, you will feel very bad and bodacious. Therefore, the contact hearing is only important for you if you wish to understand the nature of the selected members.

12.   Us versus them

This slogan will make you understand that the entire slogan of unity will forever haunt you. The brainwashing gets its momentum when it is trending at a larger scale and there is a policy of us contamination with the them syndrome. This means that the US is not able to engage the them processors and with the passage of time, the people are able to have a strong fan page about it.

13.   Lie less and do more

The deceiving personality knows that he has to make sure of his conversations. If he lies more and more then he will get under the curve of badness and with the passage of time, he will feel himself to be bad. Also, there is a chance of him to get caught and could end himself in a bad manner. Therefore, in deception, the manipulator lies less and less and gets away from it.

14.   Telling the truth in a misleading manner

Telling the truth in a misleading manner means that one has to be very effective in its regard. The telling of truth in a misleading manner showcases the strength of personalities and hence, the people are able to be maneuvered in a better way. Therefore, the deceiving personality uses the edifice of deception to make sure that the individual is all bad and worse in the frame.

15.   The deceiver knows his target

The deceiver always does his best in knowing the target in an effective manner and when he approaches in an acute way, he tends to be very effective and efficacious in its rating. Therefore, the use of deception is a tool to know the target effectively and the time taken for its progress will also be used in a longer way.

16. Keep your facts straight

The keeping of facts straight makes you understand that what are the uses of fact measures. The idea is simply that the deceiving personality uses the facts straight and effective in its regard and with the passage of time, the facts are quite pertinent in its regard. Therefore, the keeping of facts means that the person is able to have a strong version of manipulation in him.

17. Staying Focused

The idea of staying focused is that the art of deception requires stealth and help. The stealth requires strong focus and assertion and with the passage of time, the man has to be very strong and sturdy in its manner. The focus paradigm will come in its manner and hence, the person is able to have a cure function of its people.

18.   Watch your signals

The people are able to have a strong set of affection for themselves. The idea is simply that the deceiving personality will focus on the coming signals and with the passage of time, the personality will do its best in making the game more astute and effective. Therefore, the idea is simple for the psychologist and the manipulator to handle.

19.   Always turn up the pressure

The turning up the pressure will always make the people look more and more agile. The pressure come with a stringent mode of affection and with the passage of time, the manipulator makes it look easier and more effective. Therefore, the use of pressure can ease the process in a curbing manner and thus, the deception will make the process more and more great.

20.   Counter Attack

The personality uses the emblem of counter-attack in order to make the deception effective. The menace used in this is that the deceiving personality uses the structure of counter-attack and with the passage of time, there is a strong version of intellect for the people. The idea is simple and straight for the persons to come across and hence, the people are able to make more and more justice to this. The process starts with a better place to handle and therefore, the use of counter-attack will make the things go way beyond the boundaries.

Chapter 17 What are the related fields of mind control?

Ten models and related fields of Mind control are as follows:

Related Fields

1. Education

Education is another field of Mind control for the people. The teacher are on dignified positions but you have to understand the mindset behind the education mindset. The teachers are actually controlling the minds of the students and they are inculcating a threshold level in you. Therefore, in order to make the things go alright, there needs to be further improvisations in you so that you may avoid the educational constructs of mind manipulation in you.

2. Propaganda

In terms of propaganda, mind control is also being used. When Media outlets use the forum of propagation then they are actually imbuing a culture of manipulation among the public. The public is not able to make proper interpretation of the propaganda at the first level and with the passage of time, the public is able to induce manipulation in itself and other communities as well. Propaganda starts with the mind control aspect and with the passage of time, it induces horror and terror in the region.

3. Predicting Programming

Predictive programming is a mode of strong mind control. In this the computer is able to predict the mind and soul of the person and with the passage of time, the individual is not able to boost proper mechanisms of the subject. It is the era of digital communication and hence, the use of computer and software can be used to incur proper programming in the combination of people. Therefore, the use of predictive programming can be used to alter the mindset of the people and it can be further bolstered by making the programming more compatible and colloquial. So, predictive programming is a source of manipulation of the people and thus, it can be attributed to mind control.

4. Politics and Religion

Politics and religion are another platforms through which mind control is manifested. The manifestation is used to contain the prospects of mind control. The politicians are those people, that imbue strong politicization among the people and they never give strong results to the people. The public are those ones that can affected by the politics of the people and the people are not able to get strong reservations about it. Therefore, politics is a source of manipulation for the people. Whereas, religion is an instrument that can be used to induce a false sense of spirit enlightenment and with no strong outcomes of it are present. Thus, the use of religion is a manifested tool through which the people are able to get under the ambit.

5. Drugs

Drugs are a strong source of mind control for the people. As they give strong manipulations in the minds of the people and with the passage of time, the drugs cultivate a sense of deprivation among the public. The use of drugs is also construed to be a platform of mind control for the people and with the passage of time, the people are able to induce horror and terror in the region. Thus, the drugs method can be very pertinent in its regard and in the passage of time, the people can be affected badly by it.

6. Military testing

This military testing is another ground for manipulation for the public and with the passage of time, it harbors strong mind control for the public. The military testing is another portfolio which makes you quite effective and efficacious in its mode of operation. The military testing is a procedure that can be used to induce strong mind control in the public and since, history it is being used to testify the allignments. The use of military operations is another source of militical mileage of the person and the use of military testing is another source of manipulation for the public. Therefore, the use of military testing is an endeavor, which can be harbored in the better prospects of mind and human.

7. Electromagnetic Spectrum

Electromagnetic Spectrum is an aspect of electromagnetic induction through which a person is able to have strong manipulation is about. The manipulation is all about the use of mind control on the human being and it has many bad effects on the human mind of the person. The electromagnetic spectrum is a concept, in which the person is able to make strong amendments in its phase and with the passage of time, he certainly gets in the effect of bad people. Therefore, electromagentic spectrum is an instrument that can be used to make the human psyche more provident and productive.

8. Television

There are many channels and pictorial representations that are used in television scheme to make the persons go very bad and ill. The reasons that come in the mind for mind control is the strong use of media to resurrect the concept of westernization of the public. The concept of manipulation and mind control is believed to be more effective and concentrative if it is carried out through picture and television plays an important role in it. Therefore, the television is a source of manipulation for the public in the coming time and it can be seen in many ways that how the pictorial effect can be used in many ways possible. The television is an instrument that can be harbored for the better use of manipulation and hence, it is a confusion that can be stated very strongly and effectively for the television cause.

9. Nanobots

The nanobots or the robots are used for proper function of manipulation and it can be seen that how these persons can be affected by the nanobots. The nanobots trigger an algorithmic sensation among the public through which the robots are able to manifest and create a stronger reaction of the public. The nanobots create a better version of interaction for the public and with the passage of time, the people can have a strong version of intellect through the robots. Therefore, the use of nanobots is a strong source of clearance for the public and with the passage of time, the people can have strong resurrections in the system. Thus, mind control is an instrument that can be used to construct nanobots in the system.

Chapter 18 What are the personal dangers arising from the use of mind control?

Following are the precarious dangers that arise from the use of mind control

1. Explicit Personality Disorders

The more you tend to maneuver the personality of others the more you induce disorderness in the society. The idea is simple that you have to make the assessment of others first in order to make the mind control an explicit target and we have to make the prescriptions move on in a better manner. The explicit personality disorders also tend to distort the overall regime of the persons and with the passage of time, the EPD make the mind controller a devastated personality. Therefore, it is important to understand that how the public are able to make strong reservations about mind controllers.

2. Health Depletion

Health depletion is a matter of strong product through which the mind controller loses all his health vitamins and minerals. The health factor tends to deteriorate with time and the use of strong minerals and vitamins can also affect the life of the mind controller. Therefore, mind controller comes with time but it is a mode of assertion for the public to come forward. The healthe depletion starts to function in an evolving manner. Thus, health depletion is very effective in the general use of time.

3. Obsessed Personality

The obsessed personality is a function which makes the system of the human go haywire. The mind controller uses a lot of functions and mode to make the personality look very bad and the use of mind controlly drains all the energy required to live a sustainaible life. Therefore, it is important to understand that obsessed personality comes as a result of mind controlling and this mind controlling is helpful in making the process go great. Thus, the use of obsessed mechanism makes the personality look very bad and in this way, the obsessed personality will function in a haphazard manner and thus, the people will look pale while reading the obsessed personality test.

Chapter 19 Techniques of Dark Persuasion

Following are some of the dark techniques for dark persuasion.

1. Foot in the door

The foot in the door means that you are asking for a small favor first and then you ask for a dark favor. This is the favor that could be very effective for you and in term can lead to a bad and obscene prospect. The manipulator would first use the aspect of manipulation so that the people would listen to the manipulator and then the manipulator would charge his nutshells among the people. This is a devious terminology, which is designed to give more and more agitation to the public.

2. Door in the face

For this technique to be effectively implemented, it is important for the manipulator to ask something, which is quite easy and effective for you. The door in the face means that you ask for something very subtle and you tend be affectionate in its manner. The asking is of polite and it is something, which is easily accessible by the persons, but with the passage of time, the offer gets more invitation and you tend to disagree with it. Therefore, this offer is a gateway for the manipulator to have his ends meet.

3. Anchoring

Anchoring helps you to give leverage on many problems and the manipulator can easily use it to display a sense of affection for the public. The affection starts with an offer and then the manipulator fulfills to price required to do the job. This pricing is a gateway for the personalities to understand the essence of anchoring and the people, get to know the essence of manipulation in easier manner. This anchoring can also be interpreted as pricing and once the manipulator fulfills the ideologies of anchoring then the person gets the idea in an effective manner.

4. Commitment and Consistency

The commitment and consistency are a gateway for the manipulator to get to know the advancements of issues and with the passage of time, he also fulfills them. The commitment and consistency are necessary for the manipulator to harbor and with the passage of time, the people are able to distill the level of trust with the manipulator. The manipulation is an important mode of affection for the people and thus, with the passage of time, the manipulator gets to know the advancements in a better manner.

5. Social Proof

This is a smart persuading technique, in which the person uses the social proof and it maintains a link of affection for the other people. The manipulator easily creates a sense of ideological confrontation for the persons and the persons can get a large sense of commitment through it. This means that there is a disembarking of an idea that is followed by all and by strong assertion, the person is able to have a strong moment of content for the persons. Therefore, with the passage of time, the person is able to have a strong social proof in the coming time.

6. Authority

For persuading anyone, it is vital that the manipulator holds authority in his hand. The use of force and the compelling nature of the manipulator will serve his interest in a better manner and together, the manipulator is able to cast a great shadow of maneuvering among the people. Thus, the authority rests in the house of officials and the manipulator and this technique can be used in many of the forms efficiently. Authority commands dignity.

7. Scarcity of Resources

Manipulators try to market their assertions in a common manner. They will show as something is unavailable in the market and will showcase its assertions in a common manner. With the passage of time, the scarcity is carefully ensured by the marketer of the individual and he is not able to formulate better postures of it. He shows as if he has the authority of all the commands but the scarcity of the resources is a way to dodge the loyalty of other personalities. Therefore, the scarcity of resources is a method to employ good means of manipulation for the students and the pupils as well. Therefore, it is essential to understand the nature of manipulation and regardless of any issues, the scarcity is an endeavor to boost manipulation among the manipulator.

8. Reciprocation

Reciprocation is a method to persuade as well. When times the individuals are able to harbor the context of reciprocation, they channel the crux of reciprocation. Many a times, the individuals are not able to reciprocate the concept of affiliation and they want to unnecessarily reciprocate. This reciprocation is done to show that how the people are able to transform their lives and they have the pertinence of other individuals as well. Many times, the individual has done something for the public and the public does not want any reciprocation but still there is reciprocation.

These were the techniques of dark persuasion and now the techniques of mind control will be discussed in brevity.

Chapter 20 The characteristics of an easily manipulated person

This chapter will look incisively into the details of the manipulated person. The manipulated person is the one that gets prone to manipulation and can have a greater version of affection in them as well.

Traits of manipulated persons

The traits of a manipulated persons are as follows.

1. They are very innocent

Innocence describes the value of the manipulated person. They are emotionally ill and broken. They do not know what to do and what not to and they get easily affected by their assertions. They tend to be all-knowing and encompassing but in entirety, they are not able to cater to the best of all beings. In other words, they are so pugnacious in their beings and degenerations that they become clearly horrendous. In order words, they are the one, who are easily predated

2. They are looking for trust.

The manipulative person can cast all types of shadows on the individuals but the manipulated person is the one that is looking for trust. He feels that the individuals do not know the concept of trust and affection for the individuals and with the passage of time, the people are not able to get a better picture of the story. Therefore, the manipulated personality is looking for trust but, in the end, he is feeling very bad and obscene. Thus, it is important for us that we get away from all the devious manipulation for us in the coming time.

Chapter 21 Hints about How to analyze people

Analyzing people is a different dimension and a hectic process in which the person's mind and character is discussed. What are the successive attributes of the person and how that person is able to shape his statements and modes of socialization in any situation defines the process of analysis? As per now, there have been the introduction of many new analyzing techniques, where through internet and programming, a person's mind and character are analyzed. It is a sort of compulsion to the people that how analyzing can be substantial in its regard. Therefore, the process of dealing with the human's mind is all about analysis and this book will deeply decipher the constructs of analysis properly.

Human behavior will be properly studied. Human behavior is a complex term, in which the values, norms and social orders are deeply considered for the benefit of the human behavior. Human behavior precisely deals with this assertion that how people are able to manifest a strong token of appreciation for others and how does this behavior changes with respect to time. For example, according to Montesquieu (1992), human behavior changes with time and in order to make the proper understanding of human behavior, one has to deeply socialize with the subject. Therefore, human behavior is a complex term that tends to make the aspiration of a human engine complete and with this interesting project, the behavior of the human will be periodically discussed.

The importance of body language is yet another topic that will be needing clarification in this book. Body language refers to the use of words, language slogans, language terminologies and language instructs through which the person is able to resonate a strong mode of conviction to others. In terms of other ways, body language is tantamount to proper resonation in the home atmosphere. Body language will always make the human people understand the concept of uniformity in the making and with the passage of time, the people are able to have a strong mode of communication with other people. Body language can be made easy if the person uses certain amount of tactics through which the body language is deeply affected. These tools will be discussing in brevity in the following pages and there will be a potent use of clarification for other personalities. Thus, the use of body language will enable the person to make the system go way much better.

Reading and detecting people will also be illustrated in this method. The people will understand the primary concepts of people to people analysis that people garner the use of body language for their benefits. These all terms will be carefully discussed in this book and emphasis will be given to the concept of reading the minds of others.

Human Behavior

Human behavior is interpreted a kind of behavior in which a human is perceived in a social, economical and logical context. The behavior starts to evolve from baby hood to adolescence and it has many impacts of it. The baby hood method is used to see the nature and nurture of the baby, through which he is able to attain a strong reservation in the prospects of life. The human behavior of youth is dependent on three modes. The first mode if of cultural progression. Under what culture, the human is able to grow and how the culture impacts the gender of the human is all what cultural progression is about. In this phase, the cultural ingredients that are the role of economics, religion, politics and society are carefully discussed. This cultural progression is able to garner most of the most of the capabilities of the people and with the passage of time, the public is able to transform the ideas of human behavior effectively. Therefore, the cultural progression is a valid argument, which gives brief institutions to work holistically.

The second mode is of cognitive development in which the people are able to be interpreted in the construct of small and large cognition holistically. The cognition comes with respect to time and the person is interpreted according to the cognition. This means that more the person thinks, the cognition process wants to be established effectively and with the passage of time, the people are able to have more insight to this respective issue. So, the cognition development is a process through which a person's mind is actually construed and with the process of time and phase, he is understood to be a human.

The third mode is of gender development. By gender development, it is asserted the evolutionary phases, that the person is able to integrate in his or her character through the passage of time, is referred to be as gender development. The gender development is a strong process through which both men and women learn effectively. The men ratio is all about rage and individualistic opinion while the women want to be more progressive and expressive in their nature. Therefore, they tend to mold the constructs of their behavior and with the passage of time, the persons are able to have more inclination to the coming time. Thus, the use of gender development is important to be understood in a pragmatic manner.

So, these are three modes of human development and these modes are able to be effective in the coming mode of time due to which they are able to have more generic comprehensions in their making. This concept is more aggressive in its demand and it can demand many overtures in its coming phase.

Theories of Human development

This portion of the chapter will deal strongly with the constructs of human development in which the person is able to have strong modes of comprehension with the public. These theories will be developed by eminent philosophers and scientists in the coming time. The individual that use these kinds of behavior were Sigmund Freud, Charlis Darwin and many more. Their theories along with their comprehensions are as follows:

Sigmund believed that every person is born with a notion known as libido. This libido is tantamount to the emotional development of the child and the child is able to harness the emotional development of libido and thus, with the passage of time, he develops the aspirations of love and adoration. The aspiration is more systematic in their nature and the child learns the wrongs and rights of life. This libido makes the child more pragmatic in its nature and the child can delve in to many aspirations in the later life. The child learns the love matters with the mom of the family, he tends to be more affiliated with the opposite gender and there is a sense of authorization of the person with the family member. Therefore, the construction of libido is a concept, which is more effective for the people to learn it holistically. The idea is simple in its regard and hence the people are able to make the inclinations in it with respect to time.

Freud also developed a structure of personality for the people. The people are able to have strong mode of reservation with the other modes of society. Freud believed that every person has its own sense of longing with other personalities and the personalities change with respect to time. The time of personality development is able to induce people with more and more assertions with respective of time. The time table of the person varies with strong conservations and the person is able to have more evolution in the coming time. Therefore, the personality assessment of the person is able to be achieved with respect to time. Freud believed that in order to have a strong goal on a personality development, one needs to harbor subjectivity in its core relations. The subjectivity could come with the respect of time and the person can learn through it. If the subjectivity is all minimum and the person is not able to have enough interactions with the people then there is no usage of a strong personality. The personality orders will deplete with respect of time and the person would not be able to make hard assertions in the coming time. Thus, the personality assessment needs to be checked while catering to the making of a personality and Freud believes that it is an important way to check the balances of the person in the coming time.

Erick Erikson was also of the belief that how persons can be elevated in the construct of emotional belief. He believed that persons are able to have sound knowledge on the topic of assertion and personality making. However, the situations in the coming time are quite different. Erik wanted the person to have an emotional check on them through which many people, will be able to have sound careers on the book. The idea is that the person is not able to make sound assertions in the coming time. He believed that the person must have an emotional character making in the time and this will help them to make the issues to make more interesting and capable in the coming time. Therefore, Erick will make you believe that the person will be able to induce more progression in the coming time.

Erik had eight stages of development for the human. These are: infancy, trust versus mistrust, early child hood, preschool and school age. He believed that the person is able to learn a lot through these days and with the passage of time, the person is able to have a strong check on his mind as well. These eight stages govern the body language as well as the human behavior of the individual in a coherent manner. The trust versus mistrust is a mindset and a process in which the child is able to learn the major advantages of socialization and ideas that who to trust and who not to. The trust factor comes with the process of time and it helps the individual to learn many ground realities of the time and human behavior. Therefore, it is important to understand that how the public are able to be shamed by the narrative of human development.

Another scientist in this educational venture is Piaget, who belongs to Switzerland and he is able to make the mobilities of the personality a bad place. He wants to study the intellectual functioning and reasoning of the individual that how the person is able to have strong intellectual cognition with a person in an effective manner. The effect of the cognition is so sound and great that the person is able to carve out a personal space of livelihood to other personalities in the coming time. The cognition helps to have a systematic endeavor in the coming time and therefore, a person is able to have a strong impact on its personality with the coming time. Thus, the cognition is a side to a person's ability with which he is able to make a strong inclination in the person's mind. Hence, it is important for you to understand that why the person is not able to have a strong grip on intellectual freedom and this is exactly a thesis that Mr. Piaget is able to develop with the passage of time.

Next comes the contextualization of learning theory. This is the theory that advocates the sum of all the construction of humans in the coming time. This theory asserts the possibility of strong cognition and mobility in the coming time and any person, who has a strong sense of living is able to have a concentrated pillar of extractions in the coming time. The learning theory is able to make sound credentials in the coming time. This theory helps the individuals to make reasons of living and adopting free in the coming time. The people want to make the credence of the personalities more functioning in the coming time and according to them, the person is able to have sense of pleasure if all its learning and progression is learnt in an effective manner. The idea here is not that the person is not able to make strong contention in the coming time but he is sure of dealing with the person float with an effective manner. This sense of actualization comes in the person when he is learning and hence, learning theory helps to deal with the person more effectively and holistically.

So, these are some of the theories, spearheaded by political scientists that can lead to the comprehension of the public. The human development is a complex manner, which is able to be perceived collectively by the humans and the humans tend to resolve more contextualization for the human development. These theories will help to resolve the function come in a generic way and the person will understand effectively the constructs of the individual in a standard manner. Therefore, the human development is a process that is able to have a strong generalization of the instruments in a cool manner. The idea is simple that one needs to be well functioning and adaptable in its current outlook and in order to have more strong ingredients of the human development, one also needs to form strong approaches to it. Thus, the next section of the book will deal with the incisive approaches which helps us understanding the mode of human development easily.

Chapter 22 Conclusion

To conclude the overall book, mind control is a heinous work to do. It reflects the use of bad norms and values in the person and it surely depicts crucial evidence of horror in a person's mind. There are many types of mind control and there are also many dangers to it. For instance, mind control is very secretive in its nature, it is a gun to ahead and it has a mode of susceptibility to the surface and with the passage of time, it can also induce havoc in the region. The mind control is a concept that can be used in many ways of mind assertions and it can lead to a bad function of assertivity by the individual. There are many signs of mind control. These signs include isolation, moody behavior, metacommunication, the use of neuro-linguistic programming and uncomprising mechanism of illustration. The brief experimentation of mind control or dark psychology was done in the eighties and nineties as well.

All these experiments paved a way of isolation and fragmentation for the persons in the coming. Mind control can be used in many places like the advantage of home court, the stance predicament, the manipulation of facts and figures, the overwhelming of facts and pictures, the raising of voices, the surprises of negation, the consistent judging process and the use of silent treatments as well. There are many types of vicious mind control processes as well, there are dark mindsets, the controlling factors of mindsets and the mind regimes of the dark. The mind control technologies are the use of gaslighting, the generalization of projects, the moving with the goal process and so on.

The use od neuro linguisitic programming is an important concept through which the person is able to have a good calming effect of mind control. The techniques involved in the world of mind control have blistering effects on the mind control and with the passage of time, these techniques have been used to induce for the worsening of the people. The internal mapping, the modeling, the use of milton model and reporting that can be effective in the coming time. The victimization of the process will make you feel very bad and obscene in its nature and it will lead to a better function of the public. Mind controlling is also an aspect that can be used to manipulate the minds of others and with the passage of time, the people come under the clout of others as well. He is all charming and has an excessive baggage of flattery in it. The mind controller does all the tricks and tactics in the concept and thus, the mind controller can give all the impetus to the public as well.

In order to avoid mind control and manipulation, one needs to be very set in all its affirmation and can be very daunting in its qualification as well. Therefore, the certain policies of it can be haunting and pernicious in its being as well. The idea of being firm and calm can take you to a lot of concepts and contextualizations and in the passage of time, there can be a lot of systematic inculcations in it. Many ways of mind control are present in which the use of mind control is done to impress a lady, there are many mental defense systems that acts as guardians against many people in the coming, the breathing of the person also effects of the mind of the public and with the passage of time, the person is able to have a sound control on its mind.

Moreover, there are the use of medicines that trigger the use of mind control for the persons as well. There are many symbols and rituals as well through which mind control are used for the better prognosis of the human mind. These include isolation, attacks on self-esteem, mental abuse, physical abuse and the concepts of us versus them. Therefore, mind control has its symbols, gestures and strong rituals as well.

There are many related fields of mind control as well. These fields include education, propaganda, predicting programming, politics, religion, drugs, military testing, electromagnetic spectrum, television and nanobots. These are the fields that are able to give more prediction and acceptability to the person as well. There are personal reservations to the matter, where the person is able to have explicit personality disorders, health depletion and obsessed personality in the making. Thus, mind control needs to be governed properly and such understanding of it can be put accordingly in this book.